SAVED BY GRACE ALONE

SAVED BY GRACE ALONE

Sermons on Ezekiel 36:16–36

D. M. Lloyd-Jones

THE BANNER OF TRUTH TRUST

THE BANNER OF TRUTH TRUST

Head Office
3 Murrayfield Road
Edinburgh
EH12 6EL
UK

North America Sales
PO Box 621
Carlisle
PA 17013
USA

banneroftruth.org

First published 2018
© Lady Catherwood & Mrs Ann Beatt 2018

*

ISBN
Print: 978 1 84871 828 9
EPUB: 978 1 84871 829 6
Kindle: 978 1 84871 830 2

*

Typeset in 11/14 Sabon Oldstyle Figures
at The Banner of Truth Trust, Edinburgh

Printed in the USA by
Versa Press Inc.,
East Peoria, IL.

Contents

Publisher's Foreword

The fourteen sermons on Ezekiel 36:16-36 contained in this book were preached in Westminster Chapel, London, on Sunday evenings between 15 April and 15 July 1956. They are a fine example of preaching evangelistically from a consecutive passage of the Old Testament.[1] While they are firmly based on the meaning of the Scripture text in its original (sixth-century BC) setting, they are not overloaded with historical and exegetical detail. The larger themes of Ezekiel's message to the people of his own day are kept prominently in view.

As one reads these sermons one cannot escape the preacher's conviction that the whole of the Bible is God's word for all time. He believed that God was speaking through his word, and through this particular passage of it, to the men and women who were present in the pews of Westminster Chapel when these sermons were first preached in the 1950s, and that he will continue to speak through the same word to future generations until the end of time.

The focus of these sermons on Ezekiel 36 will be familiar to those who have read some of the other published works of Dr Lloyd-Jones, *viz.* the unchanging, recurring needs of human

---

[1] *Old Testament Evangelistic Sermons* (Edinburgh: Banner of Truth Trust, 1995) contains sermons on isolated texts.

beings *and* the everlasting good news of God's grace. The
'Doctor' dealt plainly with the reality of sin as disobedience to
God's law, as rebellion, perversity, corruption, ignorance, guilt
and condemnation; but he also exulted in the tenderness and
abundance of God's salvation, pardon and cleansing through
the life, death, and resurrection of Jesus Christ, the incar-
nate Son of God. It was his focus on such crucially important
gospel truths—that we sinners are 'saved by grace alone'—
that made his preaching, and these sermons on Ezekiel 36,
truly timeless.

THE PUBLISHER
September 2018

1. The Revelation from God

Moreover the word of the LORD came unto me, saying ...
—Ezekiel 36:16

WE begin our study of Ezekiel 36:16-38 by concentrating on this introductory statement in verse 16 and by means of it having a general look at the entire passage. Now the first thing that strikes anybody who is familiar with the Bible is that the phrase in verse 16 is one that is found in many places in the Bible. Indeed, it is one of the most characteristic statements of the prophecies recorded by Ezekiel, Jeremiah, Isaiah and the other prophets in the Old Testament: 'The word of the Lord came unto me, saying ...'—and then follows the message. And here it seems to me that the message of the entire book of Ezekiel is presented to us very clearly and plainly in these verses.

The context is always interesting. When this word of God came to Ezekiel, the children of Israel were not only in trouble; they were in captivity. Ezekiel was one of the prophets who wrote in the midst of captivity. Some of the other prophets, like Isaiah and Jeremiah, wrote before the captivity, while the children of Israel were still in their land. But by the time Ezekiel came, the calamity had happened; nemesis had descended upon them. Their great city was a mess of rubble

I

and they had been carried away as captives by the Chaldeans to the land of Babylon.

While in the misery of captivity they had time to consider their whole situation, and as they looked back, this is what they found. Things had been all right with them for a while; they had been put into their land by God and they had experienced blessing and prosperity. But then things had begun to go wrong.

In that situation they were addressed by a number of people. Men whom they called prophets—teachers who claimed to be profound students of affairs and of history—declared that, as the result of their study and meditations, they were able to offer advice to the people. Their message was, in effect, that though things were not all right, there was nothing to be alarmed about. If the people made a slight modification here and there, all would be well with them.

On the other hand, there were certain men who claimed that they had been specially called and sent by God—men like Isaiah, Jeremiah and the others whose works are recorded in the Old Testament canon. They said something very different: that the situation was desperately serious and that, unless the nation repented in sackcloth and ashes, calamity was bound to come. Their message is typified by a phrase uttered by the prophet Joel: 'Rend your heart, and not your garments, and turn unto the LORD your God' (Joel 2:13). The situation, said these men, was so desperately urgent that nothing but an essential renovation, a complete humbling before God and a turning back to him, could save them.

There was a great quarrel going on between these two groups. The false prophets ridiculed the true prophets and comforted the people; and the people sat at ease in Zion. 'They rested on their lees', as the picturesque expression puts it. They carried on enjoying themselves, some of them lying on ivory beds, indulging in luxury and living for sheer pleasure, drink and dancing. The position continued to degenerate from bad to worse, until at last the predictions of the true prophets were fulfilled literally and the Chaldean host came and demolished the city of Jerusalem, and carried away the people captive into the land of Babylon.

That was what the people saw when they looked back. And here they were now, in this land of Babylon, by strange waters, 'down and out', as it were; finished. What hope was there for them? What could they do? They no longer wanted to hear the easy, smooth words of the false prophets; at last, they had seen through them. But what could they do? They were weak and helpless. They did not know where to turn. How could they ever get back to their land and to their great city of Jerusalem? They were disgraced, humbled and humiliated in the sight of all the nations around them. What hope was there for them as a people?

There was no hope, apart from the words of our text. This is how it came to them. There was a man amongst them called Ezekiel to whom the word of the Lord came suddenly. This was not the first time it had come; if you read his whole book you will find that it came repeatedly. He was with them as a captive; he sat down amongst them, in their misery and shame, by the waters of Babylon. But into this situation of utter hopelessness the word of the Lord came to him, opening a door, giving hope and showing a way of deliverance.

This is so typical of the whole biblical message. It is precisely what the Bible does at all times and in all generations, including today, because surely our situation is strangely analogous to that of the children of Israel in the helplessness and hopelessness of their captivity in Babylon. Look at our history: there is an exact repetition of what I have just been describing. Final disaster has not overtaken us nor our world, but we are in trouble.

The whole question is, what is the matter? Again, we see the same division as in Israel's day. We pick up our newspapers and we look at their front pages, and we scarcely know what to think. Is the world in trouble or not? From the latest news, the things that are given prominence, it seems there cannot be anything wrong with the world; why, everything's wonderful! Let's have a good time! The general impression given is, 'No, no, there's nothing very serious about it all.' These are the voices that are speaking to modern men and women. They have a feeling that something is wrong, yet they listen to these various voices and they find it very difficult to know whether they really ought to take things seriously or not. So much focus is given to sheer pleasure, to that which is animal, to sheer sport, that they think the situation cannot be serious.

There are many other voices, such as the one that comes to us through the radio. We listen to its programmes and say, 'Well now, let's see: how much is there here which is serious?' There is very little. Most of it is sheer entertainment: we are told to laugh and to have a marvellous time together. There does not seem to be anything serious after all, so why should we be troubled?

Then there is the word of the politician: confused and uncertain, not seeming to know which way to turn or what to do; and there are the words of the philosophers and of poets. All of them, when put together, leave us with the impression that, while there is a problem, there is nothing really desperately wrong. Above all, there is no line given; there is no door of hope opening before us. What can we expect? Have we any prospect of anything better?

What do you make of it all as you listen to these various voices that come to you from different directions? Is it not all confusion? Is it not a repetition of this old story: at ease in Zion, people still thinking mainly of having their supposed good time, spending all their money, getting things while they can, living for the moment, hand to mouth, day to day?

Thus we are confronted by this baffling situation. And were it not that we still have this word from the Lord, there would be no hope at all. But here it is: the message that keeps on coming, as it did in Israel's day and as it always has done.

The tragedy is that the vast majority of people seem to be heedless and unconcerned about this message. They feel that it is irrelevant. The main thing to do, they say, is to follow the latest news: 'That's the relevant thing. The Bible, well, it's just an old book, it's old fashioned and out of date. It's got nothing to say to us now.' So they look in every direction except in the direction of God's word, exactly as the children of Israel did.

Why should we listen to the Bible? When we consider a Bible passage, are we doing something wise or foolish? Are we simply perpetuating an ancient custom? Or is this the most relevant word coming to humanity in its confusion today? Surely nothing is more important for us than our whole approach to this book. So many people are not Christian and are in trouble, and they are missing the glories of this salvation because their whole attitude to this word is wrong. So why should we listen to this particular message?

The fundamental reason for listening to this message and paying attention to it is because it is a revelation from God: 'Moreover the word of the LORD came unto me, saying ...' It is unique. It is in a different category from everything else.

It is not a part of the preaching of the gospel to disparage everything else in and of itself. But we are entitled to say that everything else apart from this word is always human: man's word, man's thought, man's understanding, man's idea. The uniqueness of this message lies in the fact that it is a revelation from God. It is God himself speaking. That is my only reason for being a preacher. I would not insult you by standing in front of you and simply giving my own ideas in this confused modern situation. Human thought alone cannot give us an understanding of it. The twentieth century seems to have belied all the prophecies and broken all the rules. All our scientific notions seem to have been turned topsy-turvy. If there is advance, why are things as they are? Why have they gone wrong?

But this message is not human. This is the word of God. That is the claim that was made by all those prophets who appeared in the Old and New Testaments. Ezekiel was a man just like all those other Israelites in captivity, sitting down at their side by the waters of Babylon as disconsolate and as hopeless as they were, when suddenly, he tells us, he was given a vision. What he wrote was not the result of his meditation, thought or analysis; not at all. He says, 'I did nothing. It came to me.' It was something he received. God began to speak to him. We need not go into the detail of exactly how he did it, but God can speak without audible words. He can speak to the spirit. He can impress truth on the mind. And this man was spoken to by God, and he gave his message to his fellow countrymen.

All the other prophets in the Bible claim what Ezekiel claims here. 'The word of the Lord,' they say, 'came to me.' And, of course, this claim to be the word of the Lord is one which the Bible makes for itself everywhere. Some of these prophets not only say that their message was not their own thought or idea, but are even honest enough to tell us that, when God spoke to them and gave them their message, they themselves decided that they would not speak it. They knew it would be unpopular. Jeremiah tells us that. He said, 'If I say that, I know exactly what will happen to me. I'll be hounded out of the country. They'll throw me into prison.' He did not want to speak the message God gave him because he did not want to be unpopular. Oh, how nice it is to be praised by everybody and to say the things that men and women want us to say to them! How nice to be always told by the newspapers how wonderful we are! How different from being told that we are fools, that we are madmen in our falling away from God! So the message of the prophets was not their word; it was God's word.

The New Testament says exactly the same thing. The Lord Jesus Christ said, 'The words that I speak unto you I speak not of myself, but the Father that sent me, he giveth the words.' 'The works that I do I do not of myself. The Father that sent me, he doeth the works' (John 14:10; 12:49). Even the Son of God said that he was but a messenger, a voice. There are also explicit statements: 'All scripture is given by inspiration of God' (2 Tim. 3:16). The Bible claims that it is breathed out by God. 'Holy men of God spake as they were moved by the Holy Ghost,' says the apostle Peter; 'no prophecy of the scripture is of any private interpretation' (2 Pet. 1:20, 21). By this Peter means that these prophetic messages were not the excogitations of a man's mind, something that man spun out. They were not a man's insight or his understanding of history and philosophy. No, 'holy men of God spake as they were moved'—inspired, carried along, by the Holy Spirit. This is basic to our whole position.

So, in our modern confusion, whether personal or general, we are being addressed by these two schools of thought: there is one message which claims to be from God; and there is all else which is but from men and women. Yet the Bible starts with what seems a very drastic supposition: that men and women as they are, in their sin, misery and shame, cannot arrive at the truth about themselves, their need or their way of deliverance.

The world has been trying to solve its problems for a very long time now. But is anyone foolish enough to suggest that it is any nearer to solving them today than it has ever been? On the contrary, the confusion is greater than ever. The world itself is proving the Bible's fundamental postulate that men and women, in and of themselves, cannot arrive at the truth concerning their greatest needs.

The Bible puts it in many ways. It says, 'Canst thou by searching find out God?' (Job 11:7). It puts it positively by saying, 'The world by wisdom knew not God' (1 Cor. 1:21). That is our essential problem.

The first thing we have to realize, then, is that we are entirely dependent upon the revelation of God. The Bible tells you that at the very beginning, and you either accept it or you do not. I see no other alternative; it is one or the other. You either belong to the people who say, 'God has spoken, and I listen and believe.' Or else you say, 'No, I don't agree with that. I'll accept this and reject that.' And already you have denied revelation.

In our helplessness we are shut up to revelation. The Lord Jesus Christ said, 'Except ye be converted, and become as little children, ye shall not enter into the kingdom of heaven' (Matt. 18:3). He said to a learned man called Nicodemus, 'Ye must be born again' (John 3:7). You cannot just stand where you are and say, 'I've got so far', then reach up on tiptoes and, being given a little help, get into the kingdom. Not at all. You've got to go right down. That means you must confess your complete failure; you must wait upon revelation. That is the whole message of the Bible: that we ourselves cannot aspire to God and enter salvation, but God, in his infinite grace and mercy, gives it and reveals it. The word of the Lord came.

The moment you begin to think of it, you can surely see how inevitable this is. The very greatness of God makes it quite impossible for us by our own efforts ever to arrive at God. Can you think of pure absolute Spirit (for God is Spirit)? Can you think of a person who is omnipresent, omniscient and omnipotent? It is impossible. The very greatness of God makes it quite impossible for us to grasp it. And yet men and women in their folly today say, 'I will understand God.' They put God on the bench, as it were, and proceed to dissect him, that they may encompass God with their minds. God is in their hands. How monstrous it is! The very greatness of God precludes the possibility.

Can you think of utter absolute holiness? Can you look at the sun and go on doing so without being blinded? So how can man look into the face of God—eternal, absolute light; endless, everlasting holiness? Who is man that he can stand and look God in the face? The idea, by definition, is a complete and utter impossibility! Man will never find God.

I again quote what Paul said to the Corinthians: 'The world by wisdom knew not God' (1 Cor. 1:21). There has never been a man in this world who, by his own efforts, has arrived at God. The greatest philosophers of old tried and all failed equally, and they are failing as miserably today. Because of the very greatness of God, we are shut up to revelation. If God does not speak, we know nothing.

Then, when you add to that our nature and condition in sin, you see how utterly impossible it is for us to reach God,

9

for none of our faculties escaped the fall. When man fell, his every faculty fell. Man's mind, will, heart: everything in man has fallen. Our brains get tired. Our minds begin to show fatigue. We can follow an argument so far, then we suddenly fail. We need training; we get it; but we still cannot follow. The whole state and condition of man, as well as the greatness of God, make it an absolute impossibility.

The Bible starts by telling us all about that. It says, 'Look here. In your need, in your misery, in your helplessness, listen to the voice of God.' To do so is to accept our utter dependence upon revelation. So the first point is that the Bible claims to be a revelation of God and his eternal mind.

The second point is that the revelation of the Bible is always a contemporary revelation, so the argument about the Bible being an old book and therefore out of date and irrelevant falls in exactly the same way. Why is this message always relevant? If you take your Bible and read through it, it will strike you at once that the Bible seems always to say the same thing. At the very beginning of Genesis we read that God made man, God spoke to him, man disobeyed, got into misery and was helpless; and God came and spoke to him. If you go on to the time of the flood you find the same thing happening. Hundreds of years have passed, but the story is the same. And it is the same in the time of Abraham, in the time of all the kings and prophets, and in the New Testament.

This is an astounding book. It is a long book, written at different periods by different men who did not know one another and who had no connection with one another; and yet they are all saying exactly the same message. Why is that? It is because it is always God who is speaking; and God does not change. We talk about the changes in the world and the changes in men and women. But if this is a message from

God—God speaking to Adam, to Abel, to Noah, to Abraham, to David and to the prophets—and if God is everlastingly the same, the Father of lights in whom is no variableness nor shadow of turning, and if God cannot change, I would expect God's message to be always the same. And it is the same.

In fact, men and women do not change either, which is another good reason why the message should not change. Look at the men I have just mentioned. Do we not see the same things they did happening today? Adam exercised his own will instead of obeying God's, and that is the very thing we are all still doing in our folly. Cain murdered his brother, and men and women are still murdering one another in various ways. David fell into grievous sin, adultery, and the newspapers are still full of that.

So why should the message change? God does not change, and men and women do not change. The situation is still the same. I read of the children of Israel in the captivity of Babylon, then I look at the world today, and I see no difference. It is a different country, but it is only the form that is different; the situation is identical. God is the same; humanity is the same—in sin. So the Bible is always contemporary. And the message of the Bible comes to this: that the one thing that matters for us all is our relationship to God—whether you are alive now or lived one, two or six thousand years ago.

You can take almost any paragraph you like in the Bible and you will find the whole message there. So this section in Ezekiel 36, from verse 16 to the end of the chapter, is a perfect statement of the gospel of our Lord and Saviour Jesus Christ. It is all here. And what is this message? It is first and foremost the truth about God himself. That is what you do not find in the voices of the world around. They do not tell you about God; they are interested in other things: human qualities, human calculations, human interests. 'Stop a minute', says the Bible. The word of the Lord came.

I say again that you and I know nothing about God apart from what we know in the Bible. Of course, you could say, 'I don't think God should do this', or 'I don't understand a God who does that.' But on what do you base your knowledge of God? What right have you to put down your definitions of God? Do you know him? Have you spoken to him? Have you heard his voice? Have you felt his presence? Have you seen him? Of course you have not. We know nothing about God except what he has graciously been pleased to reveal and to manifest to us. And what he has revealed is clear. He is a holy God. Read the Ten Commandments and there you will have some inkling of God. He is the Maker, the Creator, of the world. He is the eternal Judge. He is the one who sits enthroned above the whole universe and before whom we all stand.

Listen to the word of God. Stop up your ears to all those other voices—to the raucous laughter, the jocularity and the pretence that all is marvellous, wonderful, thrilling, exciting. Shut it out and begin to listen to what God tells you about himself. He tells you about his eternal glory. Then he tells you about God creating the world and creating man and woman. You must start with these things. Then he goes on to tell you the truth about men and women. The tragedy of listening to the voices from the world around is that they do not tell us the truth about ourselves!

Read your newspapers; what do they tell you that man is? I suggest that the only conclusion you can come to is that man is an animal, and that the most important things for man are food, drink and sex. The impression given is that man is a creature of the jungle, a mass of complexes, a kind of beast that does not know what to do with himself.

Oh, begin to listen to the word of God that will tell you the truth about yourself! Man was never meant to be as he is. What you see depicted in the newspapers was never meant to be life! That is not life—that is hell! That is what we have made of life.

It is only in the Bible that you realize the greatness and the glory of man: his true nature, what he was meant for, what his life was designed for, what he was intended to be and to do. Listen to the truth about yourself as you find it here. Likewise you will find the truth about history and about eternity. You will find it all. But the particular question that this paragraph in Ezekiel will make us concentrate on, as we come to deal with it in detail, is: why is man as he is?

Let me give you a foretaste of the answer. Listen to how it is put in the next verse: 'Son of man, when the house of Israel dwelt in their own land, they defiled it by their own way and by their doings' (Ezek. 36:17). That was why things were as they were in Israel. It was as if God had said to Ezekiel, 'Ezekiel, you are sitting with your contemporaries, your fellow countrymen, by the waters of Babylon, and you are all miserable and unhappy. But the question is: why are you here instead of being in Israel? The answer is quite plain: it's your own folly. You polluted your own land. You defiled it. You rebelled against God and his ways. You brought this upon yourselves. It's you who are the cause; not your circumstances, nor anything else. You have done it yourself.' And then God said that he hated what they had done and condemned it, to the extent that he punished it; and that it was he who, through the Chaldeans, had flung them out of their own land and amongst the nations. You cannot trifle with God, and neither can you escape him. God punishes sin; he has done so from the very beginning. As he threw Adam and

Eve out of the garden of Eden, so he threw his own people out of the land of Israel.

But, oh, thank God, it does not stop there: 'The word of the LORD came unto me, saying …' After the message had told the people about God and about themselves, why they were where they were and why God had punished them, it went on to tell them that, in spite of it all, God would deliver them — not because they deserved it, but for the sake of his own glory and his own name.

'The word of the LORD came.' The glory of this book is that it keeps on saying that! You and I, had we been in the position of God, would have dismissed these children of Israel repeatedly out of our sight. But God came down to them and spoke to them.

This is the whole message of the gospel. When the fullness of the times had come, God sent forth his own Son — the Word of God himself, the expression of God's love, God's final word to man in the person of his only Son. He came and he spoke and he did. And the bread and the wine still speak. They are all speaking the same message: God's way of deliverance for us in spite of ourselves.

Finally, in the light of all this, *God's word calls us to repent, to think again*. God said to Ezekiel, 'Go and tell those people that; when they see it, they'll hate themselves and their sins. They'll abominate themselves. Call them to repentance and to turn back to me.' That is the Bible's message. It is a complete message, which must be accepted as a whole. You cannot pick out parts of it and say, 'I'll take that and leave out the rest.' That is impossible. This is a revelation from God. It is not what men and women have discovered; it is what God has revealed concerning himself. If I accept it as revelation, I must, to be consistent and logical, accept it all.

But you say, 'I don't like that doctrine of sin.' I am not asking you what you like; I am asking you to believe what God has said. But if you do not start by accepting what the Bible tells you about the holiness of God, you will never know his love. The false prophets said to Israel, 'Ah, it's all right! God is love. Don't take this too seriously! Carry on. God is love.' But they found that God was also just, and that is why they were carried away to Babylon. Yes, God is love. But God is holy. God is light, and in him is no darkness at all. You must take the whole message.

You say, 'But it seems to me to be rather degrading to ask a man to admit that he's a miserable, vile sinner. I don't believe that sort of stuff.' Again, I say that it is not a question of what you like. When you really get to know yourself, you will see that it is true. But even until that point, believe it because it is God's diagnosis of you. It is what God has revealed. No man has ever known Christ as his Saviour until he has known his need of a Saviour. That was the whole trouble with the Pharisees: they did not like to think that they were sinners. They did not like to see their need of a Saviour, so they rejected Christ. It is those who see their need who thank God for their salvation. You cannot pick and choose in this salvation. It is an entire message, and every single part must be taken. If you do not take it all together, what you think is gospel is something else.

There are people who hate the doctrine of the blood of Christ. They say, 'I don't like this insistence upon the blood.' If you do not like it, I cannot help it—but you will never go to heaven without it. There is only one way of entering into the holiest of all, and that is by the blood of Jesus Christ. Without the shedding of blood there is no remission of sins. That was not an idea concocted by the prophets or by any priest; it was a revelation of God. God called Moses up onto the mountain and said, 'Listen, I want to give you a pattern of the tabernacle and offerings.' He told him all about which animals to take and which to reject, how the priests were to put their hands on the animal, how to slay it, how to burn the carcass and how to offer the blood. The message must all be taken together as a whole.

I end by putting the gospel message in this way to any troubled or unhappy soul. You are like Ezekiel. You are sitting in shame and sorrow. You had your ideas about life and about what you could do. You thought you had a strong will and that you could play with sin. But you have discovered that it was sin that was playing with you, and you have lost your character and your reputation. You feel you have discovered at last that you cannot master things. You are down and you are in shame, sitting by the waters of Babylon.

Listen: can you not hear the word of God speaking to you and telling you that, in spite of all your folly, arrogance and shame that you have brought down upon yourself, yet, for his own name's sake, God sent his Son into the world to die for you and for your sins? He comes to you just where you are, sitting by the waters of Babylon in the midst of your failure and degradation. He tells you why you are there. And he tells you how he can lift you out of it and take you back to himself, cleanse you, wash you, fill you with his Spirit, give you a new heart, a heart of flesh, and shower his mighty blessings upon you.

Have you heard him? Has the word of God in Jesus Christ come to you? That is what he is saying. 'God so loved the world, that he gave his only begotten Son, that *whosoever* believeth in him should not perish, but have everlasting life' (John 3:16). Listen!

2. The Act of Rebellion

Moreover the word of the LORD came unto me, saying, Son of man, when the house of Israel dwelt in their own land, they defiled it by their own way and by their doings: their way was before me as the uncleanness of a removed woman. Wherefore I poured my fury upon them for the blood that they had shed upon the land, and for their idols wherewith they had polluted it: and I scattered them among the heathen, and they were dispersed through the countries: according to their way and according to their doings I judged them. And when they entered unto the heathen, whither they went, they profaned my holy name, when they said to them, These are the people of the LORD, and are gone forth out of his land. —Ezekiel 36:16-20

THE children of Israel are in trouble. A powerful enemy came and invaded their land, smashed down the walls and the ramparts of their great city Jerusalem, smashed their noble buildings including the temple, left the place a heap of rubble and carried away the people to their own country of Babylon. And here they are now, the children of Israel, in Babylon, in captivity. And amongst them is this man Ezekiel, the prophet of God, sitting down by their side, as one of them, by the waters of Babylon. They sometimes look back and think of their own country and the city of Jerusalem, and they wonder why they are where they are. And it is in this situation that God gave this message to his prophet Ezekiel to deliver to this captive people.

We indicated that here we have a most typical biblical statement. The fact is, there is only one message in the Bible from beginning to end, put in different ways at different times with different pictures and illustrations. It is the message that comes from God.

This book is not a human book. It is not man's ideas. It is the word of the Lord. Ezekiel had not been spending weeks and months in study, trying to understand the situation, and at last felt that he had discovered it and went to address the people; not at all. While he was sitting in helplessness and hopelessness with his fellow countrymen, the word of the Lord came to him. And that is still the only hope for our world. The word that comes to the world today is precisely this old word. Here is a perfect summary of the gospel.

We noted how this message is a complete whole. It has got parts, but the parts are parts of a whole. And there is nothing more vital for us to grasp at the very beginning than this: we either accept this message as a whole, or else we do not accept it. You cannot take it in bits and portions.

The glory of this biblical message is that each step leads to another. The parts are not disparate or unrelated. I have often said that if I had no other reason for believing that this is the word of God, its logic alone would have been enough for me. It starts with a position, and it goes from there to the next step, and then to the next. And it is always a logical whole, a perfect piece. And if we do not accept every single part, we will never know the whole and we will never experience the great salvation that it has to give us.

So the word of the Lord comes to Ezekiel, and the first thing it deals with is this: why are things as they are? That was the first thing that God told the prophet Ezekiel to say to the captive children of Israel. It is an obvious thing to do: you start with people where they are and you ask the obvious question. What are the children of Israel doing in Babylon? Why are you not back in your own country? Why are you not in the city of Jerusalem? What are you doing here? It investigates that and pronounces God's judgment upon it.

Whether we like it or not, the Bible always starts there. I am well aware that modern men and women do not like that. They say, 'You know, you needn't spend any time in diagnosing me and in talking about sin. Give me the remedy.' They want to be healed quickly. They do not like to be probed and searched and shown to themselves as they really are. They say, 'There's no need for all that. Just tell me about the love of God and how everything can be put right in a second. That's what I want.'

But God does not do it like that. He starts with us where we are. You are in Babylon. What are you doing there? How did you ever come to be there? There is no return until we see clearly why we have ever got there.

Why are men and women what they are? Why is the world as it is today? What is the explanation of this trouble? The Bible always starts here, and this seems to me so self-evident that frankly I find it very difficult to understand the mentality that objects to it. Of course, you may prefer the sort of doctor who, when you are ill, comes into your bedroom and without examining you at all says, 'I hear that you've got pain. Very well, I'll give you a shot of morphia.' And the pain is gone, you feel perfectly happy and all is well. And this pleasant doctor, who has not wasted any time at all in examining you and searching you, does it quickly and off he goes.

If you do prefer that sort of doctor, I can assure you that you are doing something extremely dangerous. Surely the thing that is absolutely necessary is first to discover the cause of your trouble. What is it that is giving you the pain? What is it in your constitution that leads to this condition? To medicate symptoms, to give relief to a person before you have discovered the cause of the illness, is not only a dangerous thing, but you are not even being a friend to that person; you are being his or her enemy. You are doing something that is dangerous to the whole of that person's life and future existence.

In other words, it surely should be recognized by all as a basic principle that before you begin even to consider treatment, you must establish an accurate diagnosis. And that may be painful. It may be very annoying to an impatient person. 'Why should this doctor take a sample of my blood? Why should he send me to be X-rayed? Why should he call in somebody else and have this investigation and that? Why doesn't he get on with it and give me relief from my pain and my suffering?' It is a very poor doctor who allows himself to be dictated to by his patient. The man who knows his job knows that honesty alone insists upon his discovering accurately, and exactly if he can, the cause of this person's ills.

Now that is exactly what the Bible does. Whether we like it or not, the Bible starts with its doctrine of sin because all our troubles are due to sin. That is why it gives us those early chapters of Genesis: the explanation is there at the very beginning. It does it in the case of the flood, in the case of Sodom and Gomorrah, and in the case of many individual kings and others who started well and ended badly. What was the matter with them? It is always the same thing: sin.

The Bible gives us a wonderful object lesson in the case of the children of Israel. That is why we have this record about them: they are the perfect illustration of this biblical doctrine. That was Paul's sermon in Antioch in Pisidia in Acts 13. He went through the history of the children of Israel to show his hearers why things were the way they were.

I am calling your attention to this, not because I am interested in an academic study of what this man Ezekiel said to his fellow countrymen so long ago, but because it is precisely the same situation today. The world is in trouble. Men and women are unhappy and wretched. The whole human race is sitting beside its strange waters. There is something radically and hopelessly wrong. What is it? Let us listen to what Ezekiel has got to say.

The first thing he lays down—and which the Bible lays down in every other section—is that men and women's troubles are entirely due to their own fault. Men and women are as they are as the result of their own actions, because they live and behave as they do.

This biblical diagnosis is far removed from what the world likes to believe about itself. But how true, how realistic, how plain, how honest the Bible is with us, telling us the blunt truth about ourselves—and yet men and women never like it. That is where humanity's utter inconsistency comes in. To return to my medical analogy once more, there is a type of patient who says to his doctor—and he is very proud of himself for being such a man—'Now look here, I want to know the exact truth about myself. Don't keep it from me. Don't shield me, don't hide anything from me. I'm one of those men: I like to know the worst. Tell me exactly what's the matter.' Yet if you do that with him in a spiritual sense, he dislikes you. How illogical and how inconsistent men and women are, in sin!

This is the fundamental statement: men and women bring their own troubles upon themselves. Why do they do so? I will summarize the analysis which Ezekiel gives us and put it in the form of a number of principles. It is because men and women fail to remember and to realize certain fundamental facts. What are they?

The first is that the most vital thing in a person's life is his or her relationship to God. That is the most important thing of all. The whole tragedy of the human race is that it forgets that. It puts other things first. It brings in other considerations. Look at the world today with all its problems. What is it doing? Holding conferences, having consultations, calculating here and there, trying this and that. How much talk is there about God and about our relationship to God? Yet that is the essential cause of all our troubles. Men and women are as they are today because, like the children of Israel of old, they have turned their backs upon God.

The Bible says that that is the one key to everything else. It does not matter how right other things may be. If this is wrong, eventually everything will be wrong because nothing can finally be right unless men and women themselves are right with God.

That is the overall principle: men and women in relationship to God. The first error they make is that they do not appreciate what God does for them and what God gives them. Listen to our passage's way of putting that: 'Son of man,' God says to Ezekiel, 'when the house of Israel dwelt in their own land, they defiled it by their own way and by their doings' (Ezek. 36:17). 'Here is the trouble with the children of Israel,' says God to Ezekiel; 'go and tell them this. I put them in their own land. It was I who took them there. I gave them a perfect start.' There they were, down in Egypt, absolutely helpless as slaves, with their taskmasters trying to get them to make bricks without sufficient straw and slashing them with their whips. They could never have come out. They would all have been destroyed: the order had been given to the midwives to destroy the firstborn males. How did they ever get out of that and find themselves in the land of Israel? God says, 'I brought them there. I gave them the land. I brought them in their utter helplessness out with a strong hand. I led them through the Red Sea. I took them into a land that was flowing with milk and honey. I gave it to them for a possession. I destroyed their enemies before them. I handed it over to them. I gave them their own land and they dwelt in it.'

God had put them there and given them a perfect start, entirely out of his own goodness, mercy, kindness and love. Everything that was necessary for them, their well-being, their life and their prosperity: God had given it all to them. They dwelt in their own land. And nothing need ever have gone wrong with them.

So why did it go wrong? The answer is that they did not appreciate what God had done for them and had given them. They began to defile the land themselves by their own way and by their own doings.

That is the whole story of the human race. At the beginning, God made the man and woman perfect, and he set them in the garden of Eden—Paradise. Nothing could have been better. It was an ideal and an idyllic life. They did not have to earn their bread by the sweat of their brow; they could simply pick the fruit and enjoy it. There was perfect harmony. And God spoke to them and came down and dwelt with them; there was wonderful communion. Why are things as they are? It is because the man and woman did not appreciate Paradise. They thought they knew of something better and could do something better. That is why they are rendered without any excuse whatsoever; they brought it all down upon themselves.

Take a perfect instance of the same thing in the New Testament in our Lord's incomparable parable of the prodigal son.

Look at that young man in the far country. There he is in the field, eating the husks that were given to the swine. There is nobody with him; all his companions have gone. When his money left, they left. They used him while he had the money, but the moment it was exhausted, they all walked away. No one gave him anything; he was absolutely alone, in rags and isolated. What was he doing there? He was a young man who had had a wonderful upbringing and who was in a position of great happiness in his home with his father, surrounded by all that was necessary, having sufficient and with everything to look forward to. So how did he ever end up in that state? It was his own deliberate action. He did not appreciate his home. He was in his own land, like the children of Israel, but he did not think it was good enough. He knew of something better. He had heard of some far country and away he went to it.

That is the biblical case with regard to our essential trouble. God gave man and woman a perfect start, but they did not appreciate God's perfection. All our troubles are due to the fact that we will not stay where God put us. We will not be what God would have us be. 'Son of man, when the house of Israel dwelt in their own land, they defiled it by their own way and by their doings.' What a foolish people, given the promised land and all its glories and blessings, ever to defile it and to find themselves in captivity in the land of Babylon. But that is still the trouble with the human race.

But let me go on to put it in the form of my second principle. Men and women deliberately turn against God and choose their own path. That is what the children of Israel did. Why did they do it? In the land flowing with milk and honey, with everything that a people could ever have desired, what went wrong? They objected to God's laws. They objected to

God's ways and began to set up their own likes and dislikes in the place of God's clearly revealed law.

When God brought those children of Israel out of the captivity of Egypt, he called a halt in the wilderness. Then he called Moses, the leader of the people, up into the mount, and he told him certain things to tell the people: 'Go back,' he said. 'Tell them that they are my people, a chosen generation, a royal priesthood, an holy nation, a people for my own peculiar possession. Go and tell them that I have brought them out of Egypt because I have set my affection upon them. I have made them for myself. I want to bless them. I want to show my glory in them and through them. Go and tell them that, because that is the relationship, they have got to live in a certain way.'

Then he gave them the Ten Commandments and the moral law. They were not allowed to live as they liked or as other people lived. The other nations could marry whomever they liked; not the children of Israel. The other nations could do what they liked seven days a week; not so the children of Israel. They were told that there was one day, the Sabbath, that they had to honour and to keep. There were certain things they were not to do because they were God's people, but the other nations did all these things. The whole trouble with the children of Israel was that they said, 'We are glad to be in the land flowing with milk and honey, but we object to these laws. This narrowness, this rigidity, this isn't life. Look at the other nations. We'd like to live like that.' And they began to do so.

It was a deliberate act of rebellion. But in doing that, the children of Israel simply repeated what Adam had done in the garden of Eden. There in Paradise, with absolute perfection in every respect, the devil came to Adam and Eve and said to them, 'Do you think this is being fair to you? You are not allowed to eat of that tree. God's keeping you down; he's keeping you under. You are not free. Don't you think it's about time you exerted your free will? Are you going to be held in and kept down like that all your life? Why don't you have liberty and freedom? Why don't you take of that? Nothing will go wrong with you if you do.' They listened to him and believed him, and they deliberately rebelled against God.

That is the whole cause of the trouble in the world today. It is from that one action that all troubles stem. You would have thought that, with the world as it is, and with all human expedients and all the wisdom of the politicians, statesmen, philosophers and others having been tried and having led to nothing, at long last people would say, 'Well then, let's turn back to God.' Why do they not? It is because they still like the blessings of God—the milk and the honey—but they do not like the laws and the commandments. And they know that to live according to God's way means to obey his laws.

God's way is moral. It is ethical, just and true. He is not a God who dispenses blessings indiscriminately; there is always a condition attached to every promise in the word of God. But men and women do not like that. It is because of this law of God that they deliberately turn against him. And though they are in their own land, they defile it and do things that lead to their being driven out of it.

That leads to the next principle, which is emphasized above everything else in verses 17 to 20. Men and women do not realize the utter enormity of such action. They do not realize the true nature of sin, especially sin as it is in the sight of God.

Here are the children of Israel, sitting by the waters of Babylon, and they are very unhappy and feeling very sorry for themselves. Ezekiel goes to them and says, 'I'll tell you why you are here and why you are suffering. It's because of what you did when you were in your own land. The prophets told you then; God raised them up. He sent Isaiah, Jeremiah, Micah. He sent them one after another to you, and they remonstrated with you and warned you, saying, "You know, if you go on like this, God cannot bless you and he will punish you." But you didn't listen. You didn't realize the enormity of your sin. But if you want to get out of this captivity and go back to your own land, you have got to realize it, because if you are taken back again and you repeat what you did before, it will lead to this again. You must realize what sin is in the sight of God.'

So what is sin? The first thing Ezekiel tells us is that sin is something that defiles God's work. 'When the house of Israel dwelt in their own land, they defiled it by their own way and by their doings: their way was before me as the uncleanness of a removed woman.' They defiled the land.

What a vital principle this is! And unless you and I realize something of the nature and character of sin as it is in God's sight, there is no hope for us. This is what we are all guilty of: we defile God's work.

It was his land. He had put them there. He had prepared it for them. But they defiled it with their blood, their idols, their abominations and all the other horrible things of which they were guilty. Sin defiles, pollutes, the land.

Had you realized that that is the very essence of sin? When Adam sinned, he defiled God's image upon him. 'God created man in his own image, in the image of God created he him' (Gen. 1:27). But Adam marred that image. It is like a man going to a most beautiful painting or tapestry and blotching it, tearing it, defacing it or throwing mud upon it. That is what sin leads to in men and women.

In other words, the radical trouble with the human race is that it does not have a true view of human beings as God made them, as God intended them to be and actually produced them. What does being made 'in the image and the likeness of God' mean? It means that man and woman were like God himself. God put something of his own being and nature into them. I agree with those who teach that the very fact that men and women stand upright upon their two feet is a sign that they were made in the image of God. We are not like the animals on their four feet. We stand upright. We are looking to heaven, as it were. God created man in his own image.

He put some marvellous powers and propensities in man and woman. We are body, mind (or soul) and spirit. The niceties of distinctions between soul and spirit do not matter; the main point is that man and woman were not only given a body, but given a perfect body. As they came out of the hands of God, they were perfect specimens. There was no blemish, no disease, no illness, nothing jarring. They were perfect physically.

And God also gave them a mind and a soul. He gave them this remarkable power of being able to look at themselves objectively. He gave them the power of contemplation. He gave them the power of mind and of reason so that they can work things out and follow the argument of God himself.

And then, above and beyond all that, he gave man and woman this capacity for God himself, the ability to enjoy God, to know God, to walk with God and to commune with God. That is a part of this great image and an essential rightness. They had never sinned at that point. There was nothing evil in them; evil did not appeal to them. They were entirely righteous, without anything morally lacking in any respect or any blemish in any part of their perfect being. They were upright and stood in the presence of God.

So what is sin? Sin is that which has defiled God's work, God's image, in man and woman. Contrast what I have just been describing with men and women as they are today—as you see them, as you know them, as you are yourself. What a terrible thing sin is.

We tend to think of sin only in terms of actions: that is a sinful action; this is not. Yet actions are the least important part about sin. The terrible thing about sin is that by nature I am so unlike what Adam was before he fell. Am I God's handiwork? Is this God's perfect creation? Look at men and women, in drunkenness, vice and adultery. Look at them grovelling in the gutters. Is that what God has made? That is what it is to defile God's work.

But that is not the end of sin. Sin not only defiles God's work; it is also insulting to God. Notice how the prophet puts that plainly in verse 18 where he tells us exactly what the people did: 'Wherefore I poured my fury upon them for the blood that they had shed upon the land, and for their idols wherewith they had polluted it.' Oh, what a shocking, vile, foul, horrible thing is sin!

How does sin insult God? In this way: it sets up its own idols and then proceeds to worship them. It turns its back upon the only true and living God. It says, 'Let us make a god for ourselves.' The children of Israel had been doing that. They had seen the idols in other lands and said, 'This is rather wonderful! They are having a good time and are doing well. And they don't live like we do and they don't worship God as we are commanded to. Let's worship these other gods and we'll have an equally good time.' So they made gods of wood, stone and precious metals. Having made them, they bowed down to them.

They turned from the glorious, everlasting, eternal God, the God of heaven and earth, the Creator of everything that is, and began to worship things made with their own hands. Is there any greater insult that anyone could ever offer to God?

But is not this the modern world? The world today has turned its back upon God. It does not worship God; it does not submit itself to God's laws. It is worshipping its own gods, and thereby it is still insulting God as grievously as the children of Israel did.

Perhaps we no longer make our gods in the same way, but there they are. Our gods are the things for which we live, the things for which we spend our money and give our time. They are the things which we feel keenly about, which we are prepared to fight about. They are the things that are central in our lives.

Men and women are still worshipping their own gods, the gods of their own creation, and turning their backs upon the God of heaven in all his glory. They are worshipping their own country. They are worshipping themselves, their brains, their money, their position, their status, their wealth, their houses, their cars, their wives, their children. They put them before God. They dismiss God. They ignore his laws. They do not even listen to his conscience speaking within them, but brush it aside. They do what they want to do. They are making their offerings to their gods, and the Lord God Almighty is relegated to the background.

Another thing that sin does, therefore, is this: it always gives God's enemies an opportunity to rejoice against him. That is the message of verse 20: 'And when they entered unto the heathen, whither they went, they profaned my holy name, when they [the heathen] said to them, These are the people of the LORD, and are gone forth out of his land.' When the heathen nations saw the children of Israel in the captivity of Babylon they said, 'Those people used to say that this God of theirs was

the only God and that he was very wonderful and all-powerful. But we don't think he's much of a God. If he were a God
worthy of the name, he wouldn't allow this sort of thing to
happen to them. Look at them: here they are, out of their own
land. Is that their God? Is that his handiwork?' And so the
enemies of God were given the opportunity of ridiculing God
because of the sin and the failure of the children of Israel.

This is a double message. It is first a message to every Christian. When you and I sin, the enemies of God rejoice. They say,
'These people said that God had saved them, that Jesus shall
save his people from their sins. But look at them.'

But this is true not only of Christians, it is true of all. Sin is
that which makes the devil rejoice. See him there in the garden
of Eden, once he had persuaded Eve, and Eve, Adam. How
the devil rejoiced! Can you not hear the laughter of hell? Can
you not hear the glorying of all those evil fallen spirits as they
laugh at God and point at the man he had made in his own
image, now in shame and failure?

There is rejoicing in hell and amongst the enemies of God
everywhere today as they look at the human race. As they look
at men and women in sin, shame, misery and wretchedness,
fighting, quarrelling and making a shambles of his world, they
say, 'Is that the creature that the Almighty has made? Look at
him.' That is another part of the enormity of sin.

But, lastly, sin is something that is utterly offensive in the
sight of God. 'Their way was before me as the uncleanness
of a removed woman.' Why is the world as it is, and why are
we ever guilty of sin? It is because we do not realize the holy
character of God. We try to defend ourselves and say that we
are not so bad after all, and we feel that the gospel is rather
narrow. Why? It is because we have no conception of the holiness of God.

Sin is utterly abhorrent to God. It is hateful. It is what darkness is to light; what impurity is to perfect, absolute cleanliness. And God is light, and in him is no darkness at all. Oh, if only we knew something about this holiness of God, we would realize the enormity of sin, and what a terrible thing it is in the sight of God! If you have a perfectly white page, just one speck upon it ruins it. Multiply that by infinity and you have some faint conception of what sin is in the sight of a holy God.

That was why the children of Israel were where they were in the captivity of Babylon. Sin is so hateful and abhorrent in the sight of God that he punishes it: 'Wherefore I poured my fury upon them for the blood that they had shed upon the land, and for their idols wherewith they had polluted it' (verse 18).

The world is as it is today because sin being what it is, and God being what and who he is, it will inevitably be punished. It has been punished and it will be punished. Whether you like it or not, whether you understand it or not, sin is what you are guilty of in the sight of this holy God.

He is still the Maker, the Creator and the Sustainer of the entire universe, and his will and his way will be carried out. The children of Israel are a standing demonstration of that. This is the one thing our world needs to realize today. When the children of Israel saw it, repented and looked to God, he took them back to the land and to Jerusalem, and he set them up again. When the prodigal realized the enormity of his sin and went home, he was received and forgiven. And that is the blessed message of the Christian gospel at this moment. When any man or woman realizes what he or she has done against God and drops before him and acknowledges it all in utter abasement, in sackcloth and ashes, and cries out to him for mercy and compassion, they will be met by the glorious announcement that God receives them; that he has even provided a way whereby all that person's pollution and guilt has been dealt with and punished. God says, 'I'll pour forth my wrath' — and he has poured it upon his only Son. The wrath that you and I deserve fell upon him. And because of that, God offers us a free pardon, a full forgiveness, a cleansing, a renewal, a return, a new beginning and an everlasting and blessed hope.

Do not talk about the love of God until you have realized the enormity of sin and of what you have done against God. That is the place to start. Are you bruised and battered by the fall? Or rather, do you realize that you are? If so, 'Come to me', God says. And coming, be at rest. He will relieve you immediately. The pain, the agony, will be immediately assuaged and relieved. And once you feel that you are in his hands and undergoing his treatment, you will feel the bruises going, and vigour, power and ability becoming yours. He will invite you to take up your cross and follow him, and he will lead you to victory after victory, to joy unspeakable and full of glory. And he will give you glimpses of a land where even your body will finally be delivered from every vestige of the results of sin and the fall, where in a glorified body your glorified spirit will spend eternity in his holy presence. Thank God for the one who came to set at liberty those who are bruised. In your pain and your agony, cry out to him, and he will give you the relief.

3. I Poured My Fury upon Them

Moreover the word of the LORD *came unto me, saying, Son of man, when the house of Israel dwelt in their own land, they defiled it by their own way and by their doings: their way was before me as the uncleanness of a removed woman. Wherefore I poured my fury upon them for the blood that they had shed upon the land, and for their idols wherewith they had polluted it: And I scattered them among the heathen, and they were dispersed through the countries: according to their way and according to their doings I judged them. And when they entered unto the heathen, whither they went, they profaned my holy name, when they said to them, These are the people of the* LORD, *and are gone forth out of his land.* —Ezekiel 36:16-20

WE have been looking at the word of the Lord that came to Ezekiel as he was sitting down with the captives by the waters of Babylon, and the first thing we found in the message is almost inevitable. The first question you ask the people who are sitting by the waters of Babylon is, 'What are you doing here? You ought to be in Jerusalem, in the land of Israel. What's brought you here?' In other words, the gospel of Jesus Christ always starts with the doctrine of sin. And we saw what sin is. Sin is that which makes a man make a fool of himself. When God gives him a perfect start, he does not appreciate it. When the house of Israel dwelt in their own land, a land flowing with milk and honey, they did not appreciate it and defiled it. That is why they were in Babylon.

But the message did not stop there. He went on to show how deliberate their sin was, and what sin was in the eyes of God. Sin is abhorrent to God. It is hateful, ugly and foul. It is insulting to him, and it causes his enemies to rejoice. And the first thing this modern world needs to understand is sin. It is the one thing they dislike, of course. They object to the whole doctrine, they try to ridicule the term. But whether they do or not, their whole condition at the moment is due to sin. Things would not be as they are today, were it not for sin.

But now we come on to the next step, which is that God punishes sin. Notice how every one of these propositions is something that men and women do not believe. They do not like the idea of sin. They dislike the idea of punishment still more, and they do their utmost to get rid of it. But here it is in verses 18 and 19: 'Wherefore I poured my fury upon them for the blood that they had shed upon the land, and for their idols wherewith they had polluted it. And I scattered them among the heathen, and they were dispersed through the countries: according to their way and according to their doings I judged them.' The apostle Paul puts it like this: 'For the wrath of God is revealed from heaven against all ungodliness and unrighteousness of men, who hold the truth in unrighteousness' (Rom. 1:18). What an exact repetition of what Ezekiel says here!

Remember that this statement is as integral a part of the whole message as was the previous message about sin and as will be the future message about salvation. You cannot pick and choose. You may be saying, 'Ah, I wish you wouldn't stop there. Why don't you come on and say something like this:

Therefore say unto the house of Israel, thus saith the Lord
GOD; I do not this for your sakes, O house of Israel, but for
mine holy name's sake ... And I will sanctify my great name
... Then will I sprinkle clean water upon you, and ye shall
be clean: from all your filthiness, and ... from all your idols,
will I cleanse you. A new heart also will I give you, and a
new spirit will I put within you' (36:22, 23, 25, 26).

'Why don't you come on to that?' says someone; 'why do
you stay here?' I do it for this reason: because it is the same
God who has spoken the two parts. I see no reason why I can
believe this second part if I do not believe the first part. If
this first part is not the message of God, why should I think
the second part is the message of God? I have no grounds
for doing so. The same man is speaking, and he says, 'This is
what God has told me to say.'

Is it a logical, reasonable procedure just to take a part of a
message that you happen to like and leave out the other? On
what grounds can you do that? What is your authority? Of
course, we know that that is what we all want to do and what
we try to do in life. If children had their way, there would be
a perpetual school holiday; never any lessons, never any discipline, just permanent holiday. And if we had our way with
regard to the food that nature provides us with so bounti-
fully, there would never be anything bitter for some people,
and no sweet things for others. But you cannot do that sort
of thing. You must take the bitter and the sweet. You cannot
get a rose without thorns. These things have been made one,
and we cannot divide them. Apart from anything else, it is the
height of folly to say, 'Oh, I don't like that, therefore I'll leave
it alone.' You either look at it all or you look at none of it.

So, then, what is the message? First of all, there is the
announcement of a fact: that God hates sin, God judges sin,
God punishes sin. That is a statement of fact.

When you are confronted by facts, it is somewhat foolish to start putting up your own ideas and theories against them. Again, this is something I think to which we all must plead guilty. Because we do not like things, we try to explain them away, as if we had not seen them. We are all so foolish as the result of sin that we quite seriously try to turn facts into something else.

It is because so many do that that they go wrong in life. Certain warning signs appear but they explain them away. Businessmen have often done that. The accountant puts the facts before them. 'Ah yes, that's all right,' they say; 'he's a natural pessimist. I don't pay too much attention to that.' And they try to explain the facts away. People have often done the same thing with health. People do not want to face the facts and so they persuade themselves that a fact is not a fact. And that is precisely what mankind does with this great biblical doctrine which tells us that God hates sin and punishes sin. But it is a fact.

It is the essence of wisdom for all of us to recognize that there are many things in the Scripture that we cannot understand. If you start judging Scripture by your understanding, it is quite certain that you will never know the salvation that is offered in the Lord Jesus Christ, because it is not only a question of understanding the wrath of God. You have got to understand the nature of the incarnation, the virgin birth, the miracles, the atonement, the Holy Spirit on the day of Pentecost, and much else. It cannot be done. We are in a realm that takes us to the supernatural, where God acts.

We cannot understand creation. Indeed, if we could understand God and his ways, it would mean that we were greater than God. If I with my little mind claim to understand everything that is true about God and all that God does, it would mean that with my mind I could encompass him and I could understand everything. I would understood God.

Now to me, that is nonsense. By definition, God is eternal. God is absolute. Even the philosophers are prepared to say that they call him 'The Absolute'. Can the finite understand the absolute? Can that which is small understand the everlasting? It is impossible.

So when you come to this great doctrine in the Bible about the wrath of God upon sin, the obvious thing to do is to put your little theories on one side and stop saying, 'Well, I can't understand how at one time you can say that God is a God of love and yet he pours forth his fury. I can't reconcile them.' I am not asking you to reconcile them: I know you cannot. But if you realize something of the being and the greatness of God, you will even give up trying to understand, and, obeying the commandment of the Lord Jesus Christ, you will become as a little child. And you will enter into the kingdom, and then you will begin to understand—but not until then.

So, then, we are confronted by the facts. This doctrine of the wrath of God is something which is taught everywhere in the Bible. If you take this doctrine out of the Bible, I wonder how much would be left? For example, when God made man and put him into the garden of Eden, he told man that there were certain things he must not do. If he did them, dying, he would die. And he gave the same message to Cain, to the people before the flood and to these children of Israel.

The same message is found in the teaching of our blessed Lord himself. You say to me, 'I can't understand how a God of love can pour forth his fury.' But the Lord Jesus Christ did not seem to have any difficulty about it at all. Do you know more about the love of God than Jesus of Nazareth knew? He was the incarnation of the love of God. Yet read Matthew 24 before you read chapter 25. Go through your Gospels. Listen to him talking about the place where their worm does not die and the fire is not quenched. Listen to him, in his talk about Dives and Lazarus, saying how a great gulf has been fixed and how that rich man in hell can never pass to the place where the poor man is in Abraham's bosom. Do we seriously say that we know more about God's love than the very Son of God knew? How monstrous that is.

The same message is in all the epistles. 'Flee from the wrath to come', said the first apostles as they preached. And the book of Revelation at the end of the Bible is full of this great note of judgment: seals being torn off, trumpets being sounded, vials being poured forth upon men and women because of their sin, and groaning and gnashing of teeth.

It is everywhere in the Bible. If you believe anything in this book, why do you not believe this? On what rational grounds can you reject this message out of the Bible, expunge it out of the book and still say you have the word of God? Why is this any less the word of God than the other part? That is illogical, inconsistent. If you say you do not believe a word of the Bible, I grant that that is logical. But you cannot pick and choose.

Not only, though, is it everywhere in the teaching of the Bible; still more significant, in view of this text in Ezekiel, is the history of the Bible. The Bible not only teaches this doctrine of God's hatred of sin and punishment of sin, but it tells us that historically God has punished it.

We start with that back in Genesis, with Adam and Eve in the garden of Eden. They were driven out of it, and at the eastern gate the cherubim and the flaming sword guarded the way back, prohibiting them from returning. They were thrown out because of their sin.

The world is as it is today because man was thrown out of the garden of Eden. The world would not be as wretched and unhappy as it is, and we would not have our problems and troubles, were it not for this great principle. I cannot understand history unless I believe in the wrath of God against sin. The world is meaningless apart from it. And you notice the confusion at the present time. People who do not believe in this doctrine generally believe in the theory of evolution, and of course they are utterly confused because world history is denying their theory. Everything is supposed to be going up, but it is obviously going down. Facts and theories do not correspond. But if you believe the biblical doctrine of the wrath of God against sin, you should not be surprised that the world is as it is. It is a confirmation of it.

But not only did it happen in Eden; it also happened at the flood. God destroyed the world because of sin. But, above all, as Ezekiel reminds us, the whole story of the children of Israel proves this once and for ever, such that if we had no other evidence than this, it would be more than enough. That is no doubt why the Holy Spirit led the early church, which had become mainly Gentile, to keep the Old Testament literature: there is marvellous proof in it of the doctrines of the New Testament. And this particular one is proved above all others.

The children of Israel were God's people. It was he who formed them out of Abraham. They had to go down into Egypt because of the famine. And there arose there a ruler who did not know Joseph, and he began to punish and persecute them; he did his utmost to exterminate them. They would have been exterminated were it not that God intervened, took them out and gave them this land flowing with milk and honey.

But when he did so, he made it perfectly clear to them that they had to live in a certain way; if they did not, he said, 'I shall throw you out of it.'

> When thou shalt beget children, and children's children, and ye shall have remained long in the land, and shall corrupt yourselves, and make a graven image, or the likeness of any thing, and shall do evil in the sight of the LORD thy God, to provoke him to anger: I call heaven and earth to witness against you this day, that ye shall soon utterly perish from off the land whereunto ye go over Jordan to possess it; ye shall not prolong your days upon it, but shall utterly be destroyed. And the LORD shall scatter you among the nations, and ye shall be left few in number among the heathen, whither the LORD shall lead you (Deut. 4:25-27).

He told them that before he ever took them back into the land. And here in Ezekiel 36 we read: 'Wherefore I poured my fury upon them for the blood that they had shed upon the land, and for their idols wherewith they had polluted it: and I scattered them among the heathen, and they were dispersed through the countries' (36:18, 19). The very thing that God had warned them about and told them he would do he actually did. It is a fact in the history of the children of Israel. How can anybody reject this doctrine?

You find this warning not only in Deuteronomy 4, but also in Leviticus 26 and elsewhere. God said to that nation, 'Listen, I am putting you there, but if you don't live in the way that I want you to, I'll throw you out of it.' And he did throw them out of it. The Chaldeans came, destroyed their city and took them away into captivity.

This is a solemn and mighty fact. How can anyone reject it? If you want a further one, remember what happened in AD 70: the Roman armies surrounded the city of Jerusalem and sacked it, and the Jews were taken and again thrown out amongst the nations. That is a fact of history. The Jewish nation is a proof of the doctrine of God's hatred of sin and his punishment of it. It is not a personal theory, but as solemn a fact of history as any other fact of history.

But why does God do this? If I may so put it with reverence, God does this because he must; because he is God. The trouble with us is that we have no conception of God. We talk about him and, like Job of old, we are ready to reason, to argue and to question him. But what happened to Job when he came into God's presence and really knew him? 'I have heard of thee by the hearing of the ear: but now mine eye seeth' (Job 42:5). The first thing Job did then was to put his hand upon his mouth.

What do we know about God? When we say that he is from eternity to eternity, do we know what we are saying? Have we even the faintest conception of the holiness of God? God is light, and in him is no darkness at all. We cannot conceive of that, can we? And that is our whole trouble; that is why all our talk is so foolish and idle. How can we possibly express our opinions about God when we do not know him? The Scriptures say:

Our God is a consuming fire (Heb. 12:29).

Who shall ascend into the hill of the LORD? or who shall stand in his holy place? (Psa. 24:3).

[God dwelleth] in the light which no man can approach unto (1 Tim. 6:16).

No man hath seen God at any time (John 1:18).

There shall no man see [God], and live (Exod. 33:20).

On one occasion Moses asked God, 'Let me see you and then I'll do this big job that you are putting into my hands. I am afraid to go up without you, but let me see you. Manifest your presence to me now.' God put Moses in the cleft of a rock and said, 'You can't see me, Moses. You shall see my back parts.' If Moses had looked into the face of God it would have killed him. No one can see God and live.

It is our ignorance of God, our smallness and our finite sinful character that makes us question and query. If we but had a faint conception of the unutterable, ineffable glory, holiness and purity of God, we would see that it is impossible for God to tolerate sin in his presence.

That is why Habakkuk was right when he said, 'Thou art of purer eyes than to behold evil, and canst not look on iniquity' (Hab. 1:13). There is no concord, no mixing between light and darkness, and right and wrong. God is eternally different from sin and he cannot tolerate it in his presence. He must deal with it.

In his sight, sin is offensive, foul. We know something of this to a small degree. We have known at times what it is to feel a sense of disgust at sin, perhaps our own sin. We have said, 'How could I have done it? How could I have been so vile?' Or we may have seen sin in somebody else. We may have looked at a poor man, helpless under the influence of drink, behaving like a beast and worse, and we have felt revolted at the ugliness and the foulness. We may have seen people doing things to animals which are foul and disgusting, and we have hated it. Multiply that by infinity — but even then we do not begin to see and know what sin is in the sight of God.

How careful we should be as we try with our little minds to understand these things! God is God, and therefore he must punish sin. He is just. He is righteous. He is holy.

That being the case, is there anything more foolish than the way men and women in sin pit themselves against such a God? They do it with their minds. They do it in their actions.

They say, 'I don't care what you say. We're living in the modern world, and I can't be frightened.' But what difference does that make to God? Has it lessened his holiness? Has it lessened his justice and his righteousness?

As people do not change in sin, God does not change in holiness. And people today are guilty of the same vile, foul, abominable things as people have always been. They are the same, he is the same, and he looks upon it in the same way. And yet men and women in their ignorance, blindness and folly pit themselves against him.

But we are in his power as much as the children of Israel were. They laughed when the prophets came and warned them. They took no notice at all. 'Ha!' they said; 'It's all right. You've said that so many times before, but nothing's happened.' On they went, but eventually they found themselves in Babylon.

It is a fearful thing to fall into the hands of the living God. And we are all in his hands. Go wherever you like, you will never get away from God. And God is all-powerful and eternal as well as holy. Oh, the madness, the folly of sin!

But how is it that God punishes sin? This is what is emphasized by Ezekiel: 'I poured my fury upon them for the blood that they had shed upon the land ... and I scattered them among the heathen, and they were dispersed through the countries: according to their way and according to their doings I judged them.' God always punishes sin by throwing people out: by throwing them out of his presence and out of the place in which he has put them, away from his blessings.

As we have seen, he did it with Adam and Eve in the garden of Eden. He did it with these children of Israel when he sent them to Babylon. He did it in AD 70 when he threw the Jews out amongst the nations of the world, where they still remain today. Though they were God's own people, they were thrown out of their own great city among the nations. That is how God always does it, and how he is still doing it. What is it to be punished on account of sin? It is to be without Christ; without God; without hope. It is to be left to yourself and people like yourself. It is, instead of being in Israel and in Jerusalem, being thrown over into Babylon, cut off from all the blessings. That is hell.

Are you unhappy? Are you conscious of a great lack? What is it due to? It is due to this: you are cut off from the blessings of God.

When people sin against God, God throws them out and withholds his blessings. That is why the world is as it is today. The world is no longer Paradise because men and women are estranged from God and have cut themselves off from the blessings of God. We have been thrown out of God's presence. We are meant to be in God's presence, and we were originally in God's presence in Adam, but we have been thrown out. As a result, we have to work by the sweat of our brow, and there are illnesses, diseases, briars, thorns, thistles, pestilences and all the things that make life so difficult. They have all come in as the punishment for sin.

And this failure to find satisfaction, this constant disappointment in things we take up and which have promised us so much, that is all a part of the punishment of sin. It is God still saying, 'There is no peace ... to the wicked' (Isa. 57:21). We are estranged from God. We are outside somewhere, not in contact or communication with him. We are not in the garden. His blessings are not coming to us. That is how he always punishes sin.

And that is how he will always punish sin. In Matthew 25 the final verdict upon the man with the one talent is: 'Cast ye the unprofitable servant into outer darkness: there shall be weeping and gnashing of teeth' (Matt. 25:30). 'Throw him out!' 'Well done, good and faithful servant' is the message given to the first two. 'Cast him out' is given to the third. And there he is, in the place where there is weeping and gnashing of teeth. That is spoken about the last judgment, the coming back of Christ to judge the world in righteousness. Those who have not belonged to him will have that fate.

The last chapter of the Bible says this: 'Blessed are they that do his commandments, that they may have right to the tree of life, and may enter in through the gates into the city' (Rev. 22:14). That is the ultimate fate of Christians, of those who believe in God and in Christ and who have lived to please God, not according to the world, but according to God's commandments. They have a right to the tree of life and they may enter in through the gates into the city where Christ is the light and there is no need of sun. But the next verse says: 'For without'—always outside, you see—'are dogs, and sorcerers, and whoremongers, and murderers, and idolaters, and whosoever loveth and maketh a lie.'

I cannot imagine anything so terrible as to spend eternity outside: outside God, outside the holy city, outside the smile of the Lord Jesus Christ, not belonging to the saints, not belonging to people whom I knew here on earth. They are there; I am outside with dogs, adulterers, whoremongers, murderers, and all who are selfish, self-centred, vile and vicious, loving lies, speaking lies and hating truth. They will spend eternity outside the city in interminable wretchedness, misery and abomination.

This is how God punishes sin: by throwing out—out of Eden, out of Canaan, out of Jerusalem in AD 70, out of the eternal city, the heavenly Jerusalem, out from the brightness of

SAVED BY GRACE ALONE

God's face. Have you seen it? This is not a theory but history; these are facts. I am giving you the word of God.

You know you are going to die. My concern is that you may wake up one day and find yourself as the children of Israel found themselves in Babylon: you will find yourself outside, without. Then you will frantically come and knock at the door, but the voice will say, 'I never knew you. Stay without.'

Nothing unclean or impure shall enter that city. Without holiness no man shall see the Lord. But blessed are the pure in heart, for they shall see God. And what makes it so terrible is that we have no excuse. The warning has been given. The punishment is absolutely just. Notice how Ezekiel puts it: 'according to their way and according to their doings'; I have punished them according to their behaviour.

There is not a word to be said. Dives in hell does not try to plead anything at all (Luke 16). He cannot excuse himself. The judgment of God is just. 'As you lived, so I have punished.' God judges absolutely righteously. And when you come to see God, as you will one day, you will have nothing to say.

Our Lord gave a picture of a man who had gone into a wedding feast without a wedding garment. When the king said to him, 'Friend, how camest thou in hither not having a wedding garment?' the man was speechless (Matt. 22:12). There was nothing to be said. God is always just and righteous, even when he punishes the ungodly. They get exactly what he warned them about and what they deserve.

Oh, but it is so unnecessary! You have no reason for complaining against this doctrine because this need never happen to you! For God comes to you in Christ now and says, 'Though you have sinned, though you have laughed at me, though you have spurned my voice divine, though you have spat upon my laws, desecrated my sanctities, polluted my land, defaced my image that is upon you, though you have lived like a beast and have been vile—though you have done it all, I have made a way to forgive you. I have sent my Son to die for you and those very sins. If you but acknowledge it now, confess it to me and cast yourself before me, I assure you that I will blot out all your sins and the very record of them. I will clothe you with the righteousness of my only Son. And I will receive you into everlasting habitations.'

There is no need for this to happen to you. The way of escape is open. The way of reconciliation is offered. It is God himself who has made it and who commends it to you. 'God commendeth his love toward us, in that, while we were yet sinners, Christ died for us' (Rom. 5:8). So you not only have no excuse in terms of the righteousness and the justice of God; if you try to speak, God need only point you to his only Son, bearing the imprint of the nails and the hole in the side where the spear was thrust in, and there will be nothing to say. 'Every eye shall see him, and they also which pierced him' (Rev. 1:7). There is no excuse. It need not happen. Just face the holiness of God and yourself honestly. Fall before him. Acknowledge and confess it all. And ask him for mercy.

And, I assure you, he will receive you. He will tell you that Christ has borne your punishment and you are free. From this moment you are reconciled to God if you believe it. You become a child of God and you will have a right to enter through the gates of that city and begin to partake of that tree of life that will feed you, fill you and ravish your heart through all eternity.

4. Separated unto Holiness

But I had pity for mine holy name, which the house of Israel had profaned among the heathen, whither they went. Therefore say unto the house of Israel, thus saith the Lord GOD; I do not this for your sakes, O house of Israel, but for mine holy name's sake, which ye have profaned among the heathen, whither ye went. And I will sanctify my great name, which was profaned among the heathen, which ye have profaned in the midst of them; and the heathen shall know that I am the LORD, saith the Lord GOD, when I shall be sanctified in you before their eyes.—Ezekiel 36:21-23

WE have been considering this great word addressed by God to the children of Israel in their bondage and the captivity of Babylon. We have seen how they were no longer in their own land of Canaan; they were in a strange land, the land of Babylon, where they had been carried away as captives and as slaves to the Chaldeans, who had conquered their country and had destroyed their city. And there they were, seated by the waters of Babylon, feeling utterly hopeless and disconsolate, when God sent his servant, the prophet Ezekiel, to speak to them. This great paragraph is God's message to the children of Israel in their situation.

Now I am calling attention to this message not only so that we may know what God said to the children of Israel of old, but rather so that we may know what God is saying to mankind today. The preliminary message to the children of Israel was: '"You are where you are and you are suffering as you are because you have profaned my holy name before these heathen," says the Lord to the children of Israel.' And the message is the same to today's generation. He is saying it to every one of us. But is that all? Is there no hope? Have I nothing to say but a message of doom and disaster? Is there nothing to add? Our text has already answered that question.

Did you notice how this new division starts? After all the pronouncement of woe, of judgment and of calamity, he says: 'But I had pity for mine holy name, which the house of Israel had profaned among the heathen, whither they went. Therefore, say unto the house of Israel, thus saith the Lord GOD ...' It has not finished; the message still goes on.

'Is there no hope?' you ask. I answer, 'There is.' There is eternal hope—the most wondrous hope of all. Here it is introduced, as it always is, by this wonderful, blessed little word 'but'.

This word 'but' always introduces the gospel. Here, as I hope to show you, we are given all the details of what the gospel does to those who believe it. But before we come to the details, a general statement is made about it, and we must follow the scriptural order. We would like to rush on to the details—to talk about being sprinkled with clean water and all the blessings that come. But God says a number of things before he comes to that. And it is certain that if we do not accept these preliminary general statements, we shall never experience the detailed blessings.

Most people go wrong with regard to this great and glorious salvation because their whole attitude to it is wrong. There are so many false ideas with regard to this gospel. People seem to think of it as if it were just one of the cults or but one of the philosophies that they can come and consider. They say, 'Well now, if it can help me, if it's got something to give me, and I am satisfied, then I'll take it up.' But that attitude is fatal; as long as that is our attitude, we shall never know or experience the gospel. The gospel has to be accepted on its own terms, in its own way.

I am not laying this down; it is God who said it. 'Go and tell those children of Israel', he said to Ezekiel, and Ezekiel repeated the words. And I am simply here to act as a kind of gramophone. I am just repeating the words.

What, then, are these general statements? Here is the first: salvation is altogether in spite of us. I start with that because we must start there. It is emphasized twice here. We see in verse 21 that the gospel comes in, the way of salvation is opened—but notice how God puts it: 'I had pity for mine holy name.' He repeats it still more strongly: 'Therefore say unto the house of Israel, thus saith the Lord GOD; I do not this for your sakes, O house of Israel, but for mine holy name's sake, which ye have profaned among the heathen, whither ye went.'

Salvation is in spite of us. And this must be the case in the light of what we have been considering. But we can take nothing for granted. The first thing that God tells us, as he told those children of Israel, is this: we deserve nothing but punishment. And again, I must emphasize that if you do not agree with that, you will never know the blessings of Christian salvation.

Now do you see where the gospel is so different from these cults and other agencies that are offering people so much today? None of the cults tell you this. They tell you nothing about sin; they do not believe in it. Take, for instance, Christian Science, which offers to solve all your problems and to make you tremendously happy. It never tells you that you deserve nothing but punishment. Psychology does not tell you that. They all start by praising you and they are out to help you and to give you something. They never first of all, as it were, knock you down before they pick you up. But the gospel does.

Do you remember the old man Simeon, that devout, holy, righteous man in Israel who held the infant Jesus Christ in his arms? He was waiting for the consolation of Israel and said, 'Lord, now lettest thou thy servant depart in peace ... for mine eyes have seen thy salvation' (Luke 2:29-30). But do you remember what else he said? He looked at the infant Jesus and said, 'This child is set for the fall and rising again of many in Israel' (Luke 2:34). What a true prophecy it was! And it is still true today. The only people who have ever enjoyed the blessings of God in Christ and who have rejoiced in Christian salvation are those who have realized and who have confessed that they deserve nothing but punishment and damnation.

Again, this is obvious in view of what we have already seen. We have already considered what sin is: it is an abomination in the sight of God. It is, to God, like a 'removed woman' (36:17). It is hateful, insulting, foul, ugly, vile. And we are all guilty of it. And the moment we realize we are guilty of sin, we realize that we deserve nothing from God but punishment. 'I am not going to do this,' says God, 'for your sakes, because you're so marvellous and because you deserve so much help. I am doing it in spite of you.' The children of Israel had turned their backs on him. They had turned to other gods and had worshipped them. They had ignored his laws and had lived like the other nations, and they deserved nothing but punishment. It was in spite of that that God was going to deliver them.

Is not this true of every one of us? What place has God had in your life? Do you live to the glory of God always? Is God central in your life? Do you start your day by going down on your knees before him, acknowledging him, surrendering your life to him, worshipping and praising and magnifying him? Are you doing so? Have you done so? Not to do so is terrible sin. I can assure you that at this moment in heaven all the glorified spirits there are doing that very thing. They are singing, 'Holy, holy, holy is the Lord of hosts.' They are prostrating themselves before him. They are glorying in him and magnifying his wonderful name. God is to be praised, worshipped and glorified. And not to do so is the very essence of sin.

Where does he come in, in your life? How often do you think of him? How often do you worship him? How often do you praise him? Is your life controlled by God? Are you keeping the Ten Commandments, living the Sermon on the Mount, concerned only to praise God in your life and to bring men and women to him? Is that your life? If not, you are dishonouring him, and that is terrible sin.

That is what the children of Israel did: they forgot him; they ignored him; they gave themselves to other things. And that is what mankind is still doing, and it is why we deserve nothing but punishment.

This has been the confession of the best men this world has ever known. They freely confessed that they deserved nothing but punishment.

> Nothing in my hands I bring,
> Simply to thy cross I cling.

Listen to Charles Wesley:

> Just and holy is thy name;
> I am all unrighteousness.

> Vile and full of sin I am;
> Thou art full of truth and grace.

He had nothing to commend himself. That is the sort of man who could say,

> Thou, O Christ, art all I want;
> More than all in thee I find.

Can you say those words? Have you found in Christ all you need: sight, riches, healing of the mind, 'yea, all I need in thee to find'? If you cannot say those things, it is because you have never said, 'Vile and full of sin I am', 'I am all unrighteousness'. You cannot separate these things; you cannot know the blessings of Christ until you see your abject need. He said it himself in the first beatitude in the Sermon on the Mount: 'Blessed are the poor in spirit: for theirs'—and nobody else's—'is the kingdom of heaven.'

You can object as much as you like, but if you want to know the blessing, you have got to accept that, if you are saved, it is not because of anything in you. It is in spite of you. And I must insist upon this, because it is only when you realize this that you will realize what a wonderful thing salvation is, and how great is God's love ever to save us.

But if you feel that you are rather a good person after all, that you have not done certain things that some people have, and that you have done a tremendous lot of good, you will never think very wonderfully of Christ. You will never praise him as the saints have done. You will never say, 'Jesus, the very thought of thee with sweetness fills the breast.' He will just be an assistant who has given you a little bit of help here and there.

No, salvation is in spite of us. And it is not only in spite of our sin, but in spite of our helplessness and our hopelessness also. We literally can do nothing at all about our salvation. We are helpless.

The children of Israel were in captivity. They had been conquered, their city had been destroyed, their armies had been decimated. All their armaments had been taken from them and they were slaves in Babylon, a long way off from their own land, and surrounded by guards and soldiers. They could not move. It would be madness to try to plot some sort of insurrection. They could not possibly do it, and they knew it. So they just sat down helpless by the waters of Babylon and commiserated with one another, bemoaning their fate and their own folly that had led to it. They were incapable of action, completely helpless, in bondage and in captivity.

And that is precisely the case of every one of us in this world. We are all born 'dead in trespasses and sins' (Eph. 2:1).

> Lord! I was dead, I could not stir
> My lifeless soul to come to thee.

Dead: it is as bad as that.

The children of Israel were helpless and hopeless, incapable, in bondage and suffering in the captivity of the enemy, and they could not get out of it. But the whole message of the gospel is that what they could not do, God was going to do in spite of them in every single respect.

So, to sum up the first principle, salvation is not due to anything in us at all. As long as we feel we have any rights or any claims, as long as we are still making complaints against God, we will remain where we are in captivity and under the wrath of God. And if you do not accept that and agree with it, what follows has nothing to do with you at all. You will never know it. But when you awaken to your poverty, your penury, your bondage, when you but see yourself as you are in the sight of God—as these people saw themselves—and then throw down your arms and fall to the ground before him and say, 'I agree. I've got nothing to say at all. I have no defence, no plea, no claim'—then you can begin to listen to what I am going to say.

The second principle must obviously be that salvation is all of God. God is speaking: 'There are the children of Israel, but I had pity.' 'Go and tell the children of Israel, thus saith the LORD.' Salvation is entirely God's. It is his thought, his purpose, his plan. The children of Israel did not gather a public meeting and say, 'What can we do? We are absolutely helpless, of course, but can we somehow send a deputation? Can we somehow ask God to do it?' Nothing of the sort; they had given up hope completely. They were thinking nothing. They saw their sin; there was no excuse. They were in utter helplessness. No, it was God who thought and planned.

That is the whole message of the Bible: that God, the eternal, everlasting God, has planned the way to deliver men and women. It was God who thought about it. It was God who initiated it. It was God who worked it out as a scheme. The whole thing comes from God. It was not because a deputation of men went to God in a prayer meeting and asked God to send down his Son that he did so! They would never have thought of it—or had the impertinence to suggest it. No, it was entirely God's thought.

It is because people do not start at this point that they do not realize the greatness and the glory of this salvation. They think of God as someone sitting passively in heaven who, when we go to him and ask for things, passively says, 'Yes.' We are the active ones, and God just says, 'All right' and grants us our requests. In fact, if it were like that, no one would ever have prayed. It is God who starts; it is God who moves; it is God who calls all together. Everything is from

God. And that is why he and he alone must be praised and glorified for ever and ever.

But he does not stop at thinking; he acts: 'I will take you from among the heathen, and gather you out of all countries, and will bring you into your own land. Then will I sprinkle clean water ...' (Ezek. 36:24, 25). It is God who is doing everything. And it is God who does everything in this Christian salvation.

With the cults, it is what you do. You repeat phrases such as, 'Every day and in every way I am getting better and better', and you persuade yourself that you feel better. I grant that there is a great deal in psychology. But it is not the gospel. Here it is God and not man, always.

The apostle Paul put it this way: 'We are ambassadors for Christ' (2 Cor. 5:20). We have been given a message—it is not our own message—from the King. What does the message say? That 'God was in Christ'—through Christ, by means of Christ—'reconciling the world unto himself, not imputing their trespasses unto them' (2 Cor. 5:19). It is God who is doing it.

We see it throughout the Bible. Here we see that it was God who brought these children of Israel back to their own city of Jerusalem. But God had been doing that from the beginning. Go back to the third chapter of Genesis: there are the man and woman, Adam and Eve, hiding behind the trees. They have sinned against God, and they know it and are unhappy; and then they hear his voice and do not know what to do. They were in misery. But God came down, spoke to them and gave them the message of hope.

Then God picked out a man called Abraham, turned him into a nation, took them down to Egypt and brought them back out of Egypt in spite of their captors. The children of

Israel would never have got out of Egypt but for God. It was God alone who could divide the Red Sea and smash the chariots of the hosts of Pharaoh. It was God alone who could divide the Jordan and destroy their enemies. The children of Israel misunderstood and complained, but it was God who took hold of them and led them out.

The remainder of the story of the Old Testament is just a variant on that one theme: these foolish people, forgetting him and turning away. How often they could have been destroyed and finished by enemies, or even have finished themselves in their sin! But God went after them.

If it is the story of the Old Testament, how much more is it the story of the New! 'God so loved the world, that he gave his only begotten Son' (John 3:16). 'When the fulness of the time was come, God sent forth his Son, made of a woman, made under the law, to redeem them that were under the law' (Gal. 4:4, 5). Again God in his own time acted, sent his Son, gave him the task and enabled him to carry it out, though it meant his death. Then God raised him again from the dead. Paul put it like this preaching at Antioch in Pisidia: 'And when they had fulfilled all that was written of him, they took him down from the tree, and laid him in a sepulchre. But God raised him from the dead' (see Acts 13:29, 30).

Have you realized that this is always only the activity of God? Had you perhaps thought that you made yourself a Christian by living a good life, by being better than other people, so that you could please God and satisfy him, and so deliver yourself and obtain salvation? Have you seen now that this is altogether God's action? And that salvation must be accepted as a free gift by those who realize that they have got nothing at all, that they are utter paupers, helpless and hopeless, but that God has done all and gives it to them freely of his grace and mercy?

That is the second principle. And the third principle is that the primary purpose of this gospel, this Christian salvation, is to vindicate the character of God. 'Dear me,' says someone, 'I thought it was to help me. I thought it was to give me a friend, to make me feel happy and to give me a thrilling experience. I thought it was all for me!'

Look at the children of Israel in captivity. The heathen are laughing and joking. They say, 'These are the people of the Lord and they have gone out of their land. They talked about their Jehovah. They said he was all-powerful, that he was the only God, and holy and righteous and just. But look at them!' 'You have profaned my name amongst the nations', says God to these children of Israel. Why does he not leave them there? And why does he not just forget all about them and take hold of somebody else? Here is the answer:

> I had pity for mine holy name, which the house of Israel had profaned among the heathen, whither they went. Therefore say unto the house of Israel, thus saith the Lord GOD; I do not this for your sakes, O house of Israel, but for mine holy name's sake, which ye have profaned among the heathen, whither ye went. And I will sanctify my great name, which was profaned among the heathen, which ye have profaned in the midst of them; and the heathen shall know that I am the LORD, saith the Lord GOD, when I shall be sanctified in you before their eyes.

It is so that God may vindicate his own name and establish his own character.

This is just another way of saying that this great and glorious salvation shows forth the glory of God. The Lord Jesus Christ always says that in the Gospels. He said, 'I have not come to glorify my own name, but the name of him that sent me.' 'The words that I speak to you I speak not of myself' (John 12:27, 49). And then, in his last high priestly prayer, he turned to his Father and said, 'I have glorified thee on the earth; I have finished the work which thou gavest me to do' (John 17:4). The Lord Jesus Christ everywhere says that he has come to seek not his own honour but, the honour of him that has sent him (cf. John 5:30ff.; 8:50). He came for the glory of God, that men and women might be brought to glorify, praise and worship God.

That is always the primary reason for salvation. God says here to the children of Israel, 'I am going to bring you back in order that I may establish my own name. These heathen people are laughing at me. I'm going to show them who I am and what I am. And I'm going to do it through you. You are their captives now, and they say that their god is stronger than I am. Very well, I'll show them where their god Bel comes in. I'll smash him and I'll bring you out; I'll take you back. I will be sanctified in you before their very eyes.' And he did it. Out of the hopelessness and the helplessness of Babylon he brought back a remnant to Jerusalem. The city was rebuilt, the temple was re-established and God's name was again praised and glorified. And later into that temple came the very Son of God.

But that is as nothing compared with how he does it in the gospel. The glory of this gospel is that it shows forth the praises and attributes of God. And unless we see the gospel doing this, we have not seen the gospel; we have persuaded ourselves that we are Christians, we have had a psychological experience or we have believed a cult. Unless your view of the gospel makes you glorify God, it is not the Christian faith.

This gospel shows forth the power of God. He can defeat Babylon, and he did. Why was Jesus Christ sent into the world? John gives us the answer: 'For this purpose the Son of God was manifested, that he might destroy the works of the devil' (1 John 3:8). This is Christian salvation. We all by birth, by nature, are the slaves of Satan. He has got us in his grip. Man sinned, and his whole posterity has been under the dominion of Satan ever since. And Satan believes he is stronger than God.

What is God doing in salvation? He is showing Satan his size. He snatches men and women out of his hands. He defeats him. Christ defeated him in the wilderness for forty days and forty nights. In the garden and on the cross, he put him to open shame, triumphing over him. And primarily salvation means that you are taken out of the hands of the devil. The whole world is in the hands of the devil. Men and women by the million are held captive by him. That is why they are eating, drinking, laughing, dancing, gambling, cursing and swearing. They are walking according to the prince of the power of the air, the spirit that now dwells in the children of disobedience. They will remain there until God exerts his power, overcomes the strong man armed and takes them out: rescuing and redeeming them out of that death of sin into newness of life.

Every time a sinner becomes a saint, the power of God is vindicated. This power can only be compared with the power that he exerted when he raised Christ from the dead, says Paul in writing to the Ephesians. Salvation is not a simple, easy thing. You and I cannot do it. Our decision does not save us. It is the power of God. 'I am not ashamed of the gospel of Christ,' says the apostle Paul again, 'for it is the power of God unto salvation to everyone that believeth' (Rom. 1:16).

Do you know it? Have you felt it? Have you seen your need of it? Have you known that in your helplessness nothing else can do it?

But salvation also vindicates God's holiness. He is a holy God. 'I will sanctify my name,' he says. 'You have profaned it and the heathen have profaned it.' How does God vindicate his holiness? He does it partly by punishing sin. The heathen thought that the children of Israel were in Babylon because God was weak. They did not know that they were there because God is holy and was punishing them by sending them there.

But God also vindicates his holiness in the salvation of every soul. One of the primary purposes of salvation is to make us holy. Why did Christ die on the cross? To save me from hell? Yes, thank God, but not only that. Paul tells Titus that Christ 'gave himself for us, that he might redeem us from all iniquity, and purify unto himself a peculiar people, zealous of good works' (Titus 2:14). Christ came to bring me to God; to separate me to God; to make me holy, fit to be a child of God like my Father. 'Be ye holy; for I am holy', saith the Lord (1 Pet. 1:16).

The object of salvation is to separate a holy people for God. 'I shall be sanctified in you before their eyes', said God to these people. And he says the same to us. God is going to prove through every soul he saves that he is a holy God and that his people are like him, and that his power of holiness is greater than the power of the devil. So if we are not manifesting holiness, we are not confounding the enemy; we are not ridiculing his charge; we are not sanctifying God's name before the eyes of the heathen.

Let us talk a little less about happiness and about wonderful experiences. They will come, but let us put this first: it is as a holy people that we vindicate God's holiness and his eternal name.

This salvation also vindicates his justice and his righteousness. It is the cross that does that. We are not forgiven simply because God is love and in his lovingkindness says, 'All right, if you say you are sorry, I'll forgive you.' No. On the cross, God smote his only begotten Son. He struck him. He punished our sins in him. The tragedy is that, today, people look at the cross sentimentally and see nothing, they say, but love; that Christ says to us, 'Though you are crucifying me, I still love you and I'll still forgive you.' But there is something infinitely bigger than that! It is God saying: I am just, as well as the justifier of the ungodly; my character is such that I cannot forgive sin as easily as you think. I must punish it. I must deal with it, and I have done so in my Son. So I forgive and yet I remain just, righteous and holy.

But, of course, it is his glorious, wondrous love that leads him to do all this. It is his love that sent his only begotten Son to die in that way and to bear our guilt, our sins and our punishment. The children of Israel in Babylon deserved nothing but what they were getting because of their madness, because they had polluted the land in the name of God in their arrogance. But God moved and brought the remnant back. Why? Because of his eternal love, mercy, pity and compassion. And you and I deserve nothing but the torments of hell for our arrogant thoughts about God, for the things we have said about him, for our laughter at him in the bitterness of our hearts against him, for all his laws we have broken. And yet I stand in this pulpit as a Christian preacher. Why? Because God's love is so great that he has done all I have been saying in order that I might be forgiven, rescued and redeemed. It is all of God, and it is to vindicate his character.

Because of this, it is absolutely certain; it cannot fail. If God had not brought back those children of Israel, the nations would still laugh and his name would not have been vindicated. But he did bring them back. And therefore, just as certainly, those who belong to God in Christ will be saved and no one shall ever pluck them out of the hand of God. And equally certainly, those who do not will go to final perdition.

Did you know these things? Did you know the truth about yourself? You pass through this world but once and you do not know how long you are going to be in it. And you must face this God. Do not try to understand these immensities we have been thinking about. But if you have some faint glimmer of a conception of God and have seen yourself even partially, hurry to prostrate yourself before him. Cry out for mercy, for forgiveness and for compassion as you realize what you have been and what you have done. Leave yourself entirely in his hands. If you truly confess and acknowledge your sin, and cast yourself upon his mercy, you will find that you belong to him; that he will deliver you. He will grant you this great and glorious salvation. And then you will be the first to say, 'It's all of God. It's none of me.'

> A debtor to mercy alone;
> Of covenant mercy I sing.

'Thou must save, and thou alone.' Say that to him; he will prove it, and you will experience it.

5. Out of Babylon into Canaan

For I will take you from among the heathen, and gather you
out of all countries, and will bring you into your own land.
—Ezekiel 36:24

WE have seen that the gospel is primarily an amazing display of the glory of God's holy, wonderful being and character. The gospel is God's. It is entirely, only and always of God. But now we come on to see what the gospel actually does for us, which the prophet tells us in this verse.

In this verse, he puts it as a whole. He states it, as it were, with a broad perspective. He shows us the beginning and the end. After that, in verse 25 and following, he will come back and pick it up in detail; he will show us the various steps and stages, and all the things that are essential to us in order that we might receive the fullness of this blessing. So what is God doing in salvation? Here it is in its essence: 'I will take you from among the heathen, and gather you out of all countries, and will bring you into your own land.' That is salvation.

Here we are reminded of the great notes of the gospel. More and more it seems to me that all our trouble is due to the foolish and wrong preconceived notions that we all tend to have of this gospel. But above everything else, we fail to see its greatness, the very thing that is shown here so plainly and clearly.

Why is it that not everybody is praising God today? When we sing, 'O for a thousand tongues to sing my great Redeemer's praise!', are you honest as you sing that? Hymn-singing can at times be awful lying and sheer hypocrisy. But have we so seen the gospel as to feel the need of a thousand tongues instead of one? Let us ask ourselves soberly, 'Have I seen the gospel in those terms?'

If you have not, I will tell you why that is. There are only two explanations. One is that you have never known what the real depth of sin is. The other is that you have never known what the height of salvation is. It is this distance between the depth of sin and the height of salvation and glory that constitutes this wondrous theme: out of the land of the heathen, into your own country.

Let us try to measure this tremendous gospel that demands such praise and thanksgiving. And the first thing that we are told here about it is that nothing less than the power of God could achieve it. Nothing less than the power of God can make somebody a Christian.

We do not truly realize what a Christian is. What passes so often as a definition of a Christian is trivial: an accident of birth—whether you were born in this country or some other country—whether you were brought up to go to chapel or not, whether your name was put in a church book when you reached the age of adolescence, whether you were christened as a child, and so on. These are the things, we are told, that make us Christian. And that is Christianity. You do not need a thousand tongues to sing about something like that.

But that is not the gospel. The gospel tells us at the very beginning that nothing less than the power of God can do it. Listen: 'I will take you from among the heathen.' And why is God doing it? Because nobody else can do it. It is he alone who has the power and the strength to do it. No man makes himself a Christian. It does not matter how good a life you live, how many vows you may take. You can go out of business, segregate yourself from society and become a monk, a hermit or an anchorite. You can live on a mountain or become a Trappist monk if you like. And you can never speak again and spend the whole of your life in fasting, sweating and praying, and put all your energy into it. But you will never make yourself a Christian; it is impossible. And if you could harness all the ability of the whole world, that could not do it either. God alone can make a person a Christian. 'I will take you.' It is the God who thought of it for his own name's sake who does it.

In the epistle to the Ephesians the apostle Paul tells us very explicitly that the power that is necessary to make any individual a Christian is precisely the power that God employed when he raised the Lord Jesus Christ again from among the dead and from the grave (Eph. 1:19, 20); it is nothing less than that.

Have we realized that? This is a pivotal point at the beginning, is it not? Is it an easy thing to be a Christian, or is it the most difficult thing in the world? According to Paul, it is the most difficult thing in the world, because we were dead in trespasses and sins and nothing but a resurrection power can raise us up.

The apostle Paul had no doubts about this. Remember that resounding statement: 'I am not ashamed of the gospel of Christ.' Why? 'For it is the power of God unto salvation to everyone that believeth' (Rom. 1:16). He knew that nothing else would do. As he confronted the paganism of Rome, the capital city, and knew of the filth, squalor and vileness in which the people lived, he knew that nothing less than the power of God could raise men and women out of such degradation. But he knew that it could.

This is the peculiar work of the Holy Spirit. What makes a person a Christian is that the Holy Spirit works in that person: works in the very foundation and vitals of that person's soul and being. We have seen the building that has been going on in London since the war: the bombed sites, and the tremendous machines that they bring along, which take hold of the rubble and throw it away. It would take years, perhaps, for men to do it, but these machines come and dig into the depths and they clear the site and the foundations. The power that is being manifested! But that is the kind of power that is needed when the Holy Spirit comes to us and begins to deal with us as we are, clearing out the wreckage, the rubbish and the rubble; and it is the kind of might, strength and energy used in the building. That is the power of the Holy Spirit.

The apostle Paul, having preached to the Thessalonians, wrote to them a little later on and said, 'Our gospel came not unto you in word only, but also in power, and in the Holy Ghost, and in much assurance' (1 Thess. 1:5). And writing to the Corinthians he said that he determined not to know anything among them save Jesus Christ and him crucified (1 Cor. 2:2). He says, 'I decided not to come and address you on philosophy. I could have done so. I didn't come to talk to you about various matters in which I knew you took a very great interest. It would be of no value at all. I determined not to know anything among you save Jesus Christ and him crucified. And my preaching and my teaching was not with enticing words of men's wisdom.' He could have done it; there was tremendous energy in the apostle Paul. He had a master mind and he could reason, argue and manipulate his logic. And when he wanted to be, he could be eloquent and moving. We have evidence of that in his epistles. He could have harnessed all this energy and power and used it upon them. But he did not do so, and deliberately. Why? Because he knew perfectly well that if he had done that, not a soul would have been saved; not an individual would have been converted. They would have gone away praising the apostle Paul as a marvellous philosopher, teacher and preacher. But they would have remained in the bondage of sin. 'No, no,' he says; 'my speech and my preaching was not with enticing words of man's wisdom, but in demonstration of the Spirit and of power: that your faith should not stand in the wisdom of men, but in the power of God' (1 Cor. 2:4, 5).

It is the same everywhere: 'I will take you.'

Has the Holy Ghost been dealing with you? Have you been aware of the movement of the Spirit of God in your soul? Do you know what it is to be shaken? What it is to be convicted, filled with terror and alarm? Do you know what it is to feel desperate about yourself? That is the sort of work he does. When he comes, he shakes people. He has even shaken buildings. There is an account of that in the Acts of the Apostles chapter 4: in the very room in which they were met together praying, the walls were shaken. The power of the Holy Ghost is the power manifested in all revivals. It is the same power that saves every individual soul.

Nothing else can do it. You do not become a Christian by taking a decision. You may have to take a decision, but it is not that that saves you. It is the work of God; the power of God; the energy of the divine Spirit.

Has God been dealing with you? Do you know what it is to know yourself in the hands of God? Have you felt the fingers of your Creator again taking hold of you, smashing you, breaking you and then remaking you? It is his work: 'I ...'.

Read this paragraph in Ezekiel again and you will notice that he does everything, from beginning to end.

The second matter follows from this, and that is the completeness of the change. 'I will take you from among the heathen, and gather you out of all countries, and will bring you into your own land.' Paul says the same thing when he talks of our being taken 'from the power of darkness, and [being] translated … into the kingdom of his dear Son' (Col. 1:13).

Here is another fundamental and vital principle in connection with this whole matter of salvation, of becoming Christian: it is the completest, the profoundest and the greatest change that the world ever sees or knows. Oh, if we could but see this! To become a Christian does not mean a little bit of improvement or that you are a little bit better than you were before, or a little better than somebody else; that you are not committing so many sins, or you are not committing that one sin quite so frequently. No, it is a complete change.

It is an entire change in our status, in our position, in our standing, in our condition. Before it does anything else to us, this gospel of salvation puts us into an entirely new position and introduces us into a new relationship. That is what is emphasized here. What sin does is to put us in a wrong relationship; we are in the wrong place. The trouble with the children of Israel was that they were in Babylon instead of being in Canaan. And what is salvation? Taking them out of Babylon and putting them back into Canaan.

The New Testament is full of this. What is it to become a Christian? According to the Lord Jesus Christ, it is being born again. Not being improved a bit, you see, but being born again. You have to go back to the beginning. That is what stumbled poor Nicodemus. 'How can a man be born when he is old? can he enter the second time into his mother's womb, and be born?' (John 3:4). 'Don't understand it; you can't,' said our Lord to Nicodemus. 'It's a new beginning.' It is rebirth; regeneration.

'If any man be in Christ, he is a new creature' (2 Cor. 5:17). That man is a new creation. 'God, who commanded the light to shine out of darkness, hath shined in our hearts, to give the light of the knowledge of the glory of God in the face of Jesus Christ' (2 Cor. 4:6). 'I'll tell you what's happened to me,' says Paul. 'It's exactly what happened when God created the world. Over the chaos the Holy Spirit was brooding and God said, "Let there be light." And order came; creation followed. That's what's happened to me. I'm not simply a little bit better. I'm new. I'm a new creation in a new world. Old things are passed away, behold all things have become new.' Out of Babylon, into Canaan.

Do you know anything about this translation? Do you know what it is to be entirely different in your whole fundamental attitude, in your whole status, standing and position? That is Christianity.

We not only find this in the Scriptures, but it is confirmed throughout the long history of the church in the lives of all the saints. This is what happened to Augustine, Luther, Calvin, and all the rest. 'I'm not myself. I'm not the man I was. Something has happened. I have been entirely changed.'

Nothing can be bigger than this change. But what is it that happens to us in detail?

Ezekiel puts it like this: the first thing we obviously need is deliverance. The children of Israel were in Babylon instead of being in Canaan, but on top of that they were slaves and captives; they were entirely under the dominion of the Chaldeans, the Babylonians, who had got them in their grip. And they were helpless. They needed deliverance. They needed to be brought out, to be taken out of their captivity.

The real trouble with unbelievers, men or women who are not Christians, is that they are not in their right place. They are not where they were meant to be. Man and woman were meant to be in Paradise. We were never meant to be in the world as it is today, living the sort of life we are living. We were never intended for it, just as the Israelites were never meant to be in Babylon but were meant to be in Canaan. God put man and woman in Paradise and he meant them to be there. But they are not there any more; they are eccentric, away from home. They are like the prodigal son in the far country. They are outside the position of God's blessing and therefore they need to be delivered from it.

But what is it in detail they need to be delivered from in this eccentric position? The first thing is this: 'I will take you from among the heathen.' 'The heathen' represents godlessness—an ignorance of God, of all God's ways and of all God's blessings. Who are the heathen? They are those who do not know about God. That is why they are heathen.

Sin has put us all among the heathen. In sin, we are in heathen darkness, in ignorance. Is that not how the gospel tells us the message of salvation comes? 'The people that walked in darkness'—the people who were in ignorance—'have seen a great light' (Isa. 9:2). Here it is all in our picture: the children of Israel are among the heathen who do not know God and are worshipping idols.

That is the first thing the world needs to be delivered from today: its ignorance about God. Why are people living as they are today? There is only one answer: it is because they do not know God. Why are they enjoying drink, gambling, sex and all these perversions and other foul things? It is just this: they do not know what it is to enjoy God. There is no other explanation. It is because men and women do not know God

74

and enjoy him that they turn to these other things. They do not know anything about the greatness of God, the power of God or, as we have seen, the wrath of God.

If they but knew about God and his holiness, his law and his wrath, they would never sin again. The thought of it would be terrifying. But they do not know it. 'Ha!' they say; 'there isn't a God.' 'The fool hath said in his heart, There is no God' (Psa. 14:1). 'Don't listen,' they say. 'It's all right; carry on. I have defied him for years; nothing's happened to me. I'm having a good time. All is well with me.' And on they go, in darkness and in ignorance about God.

Oh, their ignorance of his love and his mercy and his compassion! If they believe in him at all, they regard him as a tyrant, an ogre, one who is set against them and who hates them, and who just delights in robbing them of all that is good and wonderful. There they are in this darkness. They need to be delivered out of it, and it is the gospel alone that can do it.

But heathenism does not stop at just an ignorance of God; it is accompanied by many other things. The heathen live in fear and terror. They are victims of superstition, and they make gods of wood, stone and metals and worship them. There is nothing more appalling about the ignorance of heathenism than its fears and phobias.

And the world today is full of these things. People are reading their fortunes in the papers. They will listen to an astrologer. They will stake their future on a fortune-teller. They are clutching at anything that seems to give hope. They are afraid of life, afraid of what is going to happen. They do not know where they are. Men and women are in the grip of fears and phobias, of heathen darkness. They will believe anything. They will set up any kind of god and bow down before him.

Why? Because they do not know where they are, and they especially do not know God.

There is something else that always accompanies heathenism, and that is the slavery that goes with it. The heathen are slaves to sins. Have you read the missionary reports, especially the accounts of the pioneer missionaries in the nineteenth century? They went among the heathen and found that they were cannibals. They were sunk to such depths that they were almost worse than animals and beasts. All the perversions, and the foulness and the squalor of it all—that is the result of godlessness and this ignorance concerning God.

Paul says to the Ephesians,

> You hath he quickened, who were dead in trespasses and sins; wherein in time past ye walked according to the course of this world, according to the prince of the power of the air, the spirit that now worketh in the children of disobedience: among whom also we all had our conversation in times past in the lusts of our flesh, fulfilling the desires of the flesh and of the mind; and were by nature the children of wrath, even as others (Eph. 2:1-3).

It is still true today. This darkness, this life among the heathen, leads to that sort of existence: the way of the world, the round of pleasure, the drunkenness, the fighting, the hatred, the jealousy, the envy, the lust, the inordinate affections, all the foulness of it all. That is what men and women need to be delivered from.

They are the slaves of sin. They are the slaves of the devil. And because of all this, of course, they are totally incapable of ever arriving at the knowledge of God. The children of Israel were captives. They had no arms; they could do nothing. If they made any attempt, it would be quelled. That is man and woman: dead in trespasses and sins, and they cannot move;

outside their own country, far away from God and outside the blessings of God.

Oh, that is the depth of sin! But God says, 'I will rescue you. I will take you from among the heathen.' He enters in, in Christ by the Spirit, and he tackles the controlling power and removes him. He destroys him, the strong man armed, and robs him of his armour in which he trusted, and sets his captives free.

This is why I emphasized that nothing less than the power of God can do it. We all know what it is to try to break a habit or a sin. We know what it is to take New Year's resolutions and not keep them for a week. We have said that we are going to be better; we have signed pledges. We have done a thousand things, and it has all come to nothing. It needs more than human effort; it needs God. And the gospel is the power of God unto salvation to everyone who believes. He can set us free and take us from among the heathen, gathering us out of the lands where we have been held captive.

What then? He restores us: I 'will bring you into your own land'. The gospel brings us back to the place where we were meant to be and where we ought to be. We see this everywhere in the Bible.

In the beginning, in the garden of Eden, God made man and woman perfect. Adam and Eve walked in the garden. They heard the voice of God and they ran to him. That was the normal condition of man and woman. But they fell into sin and disobedience, and when God came down into the garden, he did not see them. And the first question he asks is this: 'Adam, where art thou?' Adam is somewhere he ought not to be. And that is always the effect of sin. But God comes after him; he wants to call him back.

In the parable of the prodigal son in the New Testament, when that poor fellow came to himself, he said to himself:

'How many hired servants of my father have bread enough?' He suddenly woke up in the fields with the swine and he said, 'What am I doing here? What's my father's son doing in this country at all, especially in a field with swine and husks? I am not at home; I am in a place where I was never meant to be. I ought to be at home.' And he arose and went to his father. He just went home.

'I will take you out from among the heathen, and gather you out of all countries, and will bring you into your own land.' What is it to become a Christian? It is simply to come home; to come back to your Father, to where you are meant to be. Let us once and for all get rid of these foolish, inadequate notions of Christianity, that it is just about being a little bit better or more moral. No, it is coming back home. It is leaving the far country.

It is a restoration. A restoration to what? Primarily it is a restoration to God and to knowledge concerning God. Paul, writing to the Colossians, thanks God for them, because of their knowledge of God. The truth, he says, has been preached to you as it has in the whole world. And you have seen it and you have got it. And I rejoice to hear it, says Paul. You were heathens, you were ignorant, you did not know; but now you know about God, who in his great love wherewith he loved us has visited us and has given us the knowledge of himself in the face of his only begotten Son. He has shown us his love, mercy and compassion. And we have got a new view of him, the right view, the true view. We are back with him. We know that he delights in pardon and forgiveness. We did not know that before, but we know it now and we love him, praise him and worship him. We are back in relationship to God.

The gospel introduces us to God as our Father, not as a philosophic X, not some mighty power away in the distance, but as a Father who has loved us with an everlasting love, so much so that he sent his only Son to die for us that our sins might be blotted out and forgiven. Oh, what a gospel this is! It brings us back to God. And as we come back to God, we are back in the place of blessing. God does not bless his people there in Babylon; it is in Canaan he blesses them. He made it for them. He took them there. He blessed them there, in the land flowing with milk and honey. Come back, he says; I'll bring you back, and then I'll again shower my blessings upon you.

What does this gospel give us? It blesses us with all the riches of God's grace, with all spiritual blessings in the heavenly places. 'Yea, all I need, in thee to find.'

> Praise, my soul, the King of heaven;
> To his feet thy tribute bring.

Why?

> Ransomed, healed, restored, forgiven,
> Who like thee his praise should sing?
> Praise him ...

We are back in the place of blessing, back where he wants us, in the place he made for us. That is what salvation is. Back into reconciliation with God as Father and receiving his blessings without limit.

And as an inevitable accompaniment, we are back out of heathendom and the squalor, vileness, foulness and filth of sin; back to a holy life, back to sanctification, washed, cleansed and renewed. Back to a life in which we, far from delighting in evil, hunger and thirst after righteousness, longing to be filled. Back to a life in which we can say, 'Though I'm still left in this world, this is the victory that overcometh the world, even our faith.' Back to a life in which the commandments of

God are not grievous but in which we can say, 'I delight to do thy will, O my God.'

That is salvation; it is nothing less than this complete change, this knowledge of God. Do you know God? I am not asking if you believe certain things about him. You can do that without being a Christian. But do you know him? Do you know him as your Father? Is he blessing you? Are you receiving his blessings day by day? According to the Bible, I cannot see that you have any right to regard yourself as a Christian unless those things are true.

But Christ came to bring us to God, to reconcile us to God, to put us in the place where God delights to bless us, numbers the very hairs of our head and cares for us with the whole of his being. He is sanctifying us, purifying us, cleansing us, making us meet to be partakers of the inheritance with the saints in light.

That is what salvation means, and that is what God does by the Holy Spirit. That is his taking us out of heathendom and putting us into our own land, into our own place.

Are we there?

That is what God does in Christ. He sent his only begotten Son into this world, even to the death of the cross. Why? That he might deliver us from all iniquity and separate unto himself a peculiar people zealous for good works. You cannot be taken out of Babylon without being separated, and Christianity separates us from this world and all that it lives for: its lusts, its loudness, 'the lust of the flesh, and the lust of the eyes, and the pride of life' (1 John 2:16), and all the things the world thinks so wonderful. We are taken out of that to this new realm, to this new life with God, which is a foretaste of and preparation for heaven. Salvation is to be taken hold of by him and to be led through the sin of this world, led through the river of death and presented faultless before the presence of God's glory with exceeding joy.

Have you been translated from the kingdom of darkness into the kingdom of God's dear Son? If you have, God bless you. If you have not, make no tarrying. You are in a dangerous position. You are under the wrath of God, and if you die there, you will remain there for all eternity. If you are there, cry unto him for mercy and compassion, and he will not reject you. He will take hold of you, and his mighty power will resurrect you and put you into the kingdom of his dear Son.

6. Ye Shall Be Clean

Then will I sprinkle clean water upon you, and ye shall be clean: from all your filthiness, and from all your idols, will I cleanse you. — Ezekiel 36:25

WE saw in verse 24 the complete statement of the message of God's salvation, but now the message is taken up again and we are given its component parts. In this verse we come to the first detail.

What is the first thing, the thing that is essential to the salvation of men and women and that is absolutely vital to all of us before we can know God and his wondrous blessings? We find it here: 'Then will I sprinkle clean water upon you, and ye shall be clean: from all your filthiness, and from all your idols, will I cleanse you.' This is the first thing; there are other things to follow and you will notice how wonderful they are: 'A new heart also will I give you, and a new spirit will I put within you: and I will take away the stony heart out of your flesh, and I will give you an heart of flesh' (verse 26). And then: 'And I will put my spirit within you, and cause you to walk in my statutes, and ye shall keep my judgments, and do them' (verse 27). That is a prophecy of what happened at Jerusalem on the day of Pentecost, when the Holy Ghost was poured forth upon the church.

In other words, we really have got a complete statement of the Christian gospel here. But first we must emphasize the problem we must face, which is our sin and guilt. 'Now I'm going to bring you back from that land of Babylon to your own land of Canaan', says God through Ezekiel to these people. But he makes it very plain that before they can be brought back, they first need to be cleansed. They are filthy; they need to be washed. But God says, 'From all your filthiness, and from all your idols, will I cleanse you.'

The Bible always starts with this. But, of course, it is something none of us like.

We all are conscious of many needs. Life has got us down and we are in trouble and perplexity—all the tensions and stresses of the modern world bear eloquent testimony to that. The way people are ready to clutch at anything and are living on drugs of various kinds is proof. Everyone is conscious of the need of help, of assistance and guidance: 'What am I to do? Where am I to go?' We are conscious of our own smallness and inability. And if we are told, 'Well, God is ready to give you guidance. He's ready to help you', we are interested in it and ready to listen.

But we must remember that there is an absolutely essential preliminary and that we shall experience no blessings whatsoever from God until we have first faced this problem: the guilt, the pollution, the filthiness of our sin. Therefore anything that offers itself as the gospel and offers to give you help, assistance or guidance but does not first of all hold you face to face with your guilt and your need to be washed is not the Christian message.

I am putting it very dogmatically because there are teachings today that tell people they can come to God and be blessed by him but which never mention this need of washing and cleansing. That is not the Christian gospel. This cleansing always comes first. A right relationship to God is impossible until the question of our sinfulness has been dealt with and solved.

This is emphasized everywhere in the Scriptures. And surely, if we have any right understanding of the being, nature and character of God, we shall not be surprised at this. The Scriptures tell us that God is light and that in him is no darkness at all; that God is a consuming fire; that God is holy. He dwells in a light which is unapproachable. How is it possible for men and women covered by the guilt, vileness and filthiness of sin to have communion and fellowship with such a being? Surely on the very surface it is quite impossible. God's character alone, in his righteousness and holiness, makes it an assured and utter impossibility. But God has also made it very plain in an explicit manner.

We find it in the Old Testament. And the apostle Paul sums it up in these words: 'The wrath of God is revealed from heaven against all ungodliness and unrighteousness of men' (Rom. 1:18). It has been revealed; God himself has revealed it. When God gave his Ten Commandments, what was he doing? He was giving a revelation of precisely this. Here are these children of Israel whom he formed for himself. He tells them that, having delivered them out of the bondage of Egypt, he is going to lead them into the land of Canaan. They are going to be his people and he is going to bless them. 'Yet,' he says, 'you must remember the condition: you must live and behave as my people. I am a holy God, therefore you must be a holy people.' 'Be ye holy, for I am holy, saith the Lord' (Lev. 11:44; 1 Pet. 1:14-16). So he gives them the Ten Commandments. Then he not only tells them how they ought to live, but he also warns them of the punishment that will be meted out upon their sin.

So the wrath of God is a fact. He has revealed it, and nowhere more clearly than in the case of the children of Israel themselves. This very paragraph in Ezekiel brings it out very clearly. It was God himself who allowed these people to be conquered and carried to Babylon, just as he had told them he would do. 'I scattered them among the heathen, and they were dispersed through the countries: according to their way and according to their doings I judged them' (verse 19).

There God revealed his attitude towards sin: that he hates it, judges it and must punish it. Therefore, it is an obvious deduction that the first question that must of necessity arise before we can get back into communion and fellowship with God is this matter of our sinfulness. And so, as you read your Old Testament, you find men approaching God and taking a sacrifice with them. Abel took a sacrifice. Even at the very beginning it was clear that no one could approach God without some sort of offering or sacrifice. When you read the books of Exodus, Leviticus and Numbers you find great detail about burnt offerings and sacrifices, animals being slain, the blood being sprinkled and the high priest going into the presence of God presenting blood. What does it all mean? Just this: that sin has got to be dealt with. There is no relationship between us and God while we are covered in our sin. God receiveth not sinners. He cannot receive them as they are, because he is God.

The whole teaching of the Bible emphasizes that, and therefore we must recognize it as something which is absolutely vital to our whole position. So the first thing that we have to do if we want to know God and be blessed of him is to realize that somehow or other this question of our sinfulness, our guilt in God's presence, must be dealt with.

We have a perfect illustration of this in the parable of the prodigal son spoken by our Lord himself. When that man came to himself and went back to his father, he did not just say, 'Father, I've come back. Bring out the fatted calf, give me my robe, produce the ring. I see now that I can deal with these things and I want to have them.' Not at all; he came back and said, 'Father, I have sinned against heaven, and before thee, and am no more worthy to be called thy son: make me as one of thy hired servants' (Luke 15:18, 19). He realizes his guilt. He feels that his conduct has cut him off from his father. He has forfeited every right as a son. He does not appeal to his father as father; he says, 'I am only worthy to be a servant. Take me in as one of your servants.' That is the very essence of the right approach, which is why our Lord so put it.

We see it again in the parable of the publican and the Pharisee who went up into the temple to pray (Luke 18:10-14). The Pharisee walks right to the front and says, 'I thank thee, that I am not as other men are.' He feels a need of God, he wants to be right with God, but there is no problem of sin for him. He just boasts of what he has done and wants God to grant him certain blessings because he is so good. But there is the other man, beating his breast and unable even to look up, who says, 'God be merciful to me a sinner.' Because of his guilt, his sinfulness, his vileness, his filthiness, he feels he does not have a right or a claim. 'I tell you,' says our Lord, 'that that's the man who went down to his house blessed and justified.' Why? Because that man realized the problem of sin. He realized his filthiness and vileness.

Oh, we can never emphasize this too much! Read the lives of all the men and women who have known God, been blessed by him and have testified to his power, love and compassion. Though they were often surrounded by difficulties and trials, these people were enabled to rise above them. The memory of their lives is a veritable benediction for us, and we can never read about them or think of them without feeling, 'That's life as it ought to be lived.' But such people all invariably acknowledge and confess their sin, their unworthiness, their unrighteousness, the filthiness of their lives as they were by nature and unaided.

So that is the first thing: we must be cleansed. But that leads us to the next point: how can this be done? What can we do about our sins? We have all sinned deliberately against God. We have ignored him. We have forgotten him. We have deliberately flouted his laws. We have disobeyed our conscience. What can we do about this vileness of sin? How can you remove it? How can you make the page in the book of your life white again? How can you get rid of the blots? Have you ever tried to do it—to wash yourself spiritually and make yourself fit to stand in the presence of God?

Psalm 51 says it all. David, who wrote the psalm, was guilty of terrible sin—not only of adultery but also of murder—and he was awakened to it. He suddenly comes to see it and wants to get right with God. This is how he puts it:

> Have mercy upon me, O God, according to thy lovingkindness: according unto the multitude of thy tender mercies blot out my transgressions. Wash me throughly from mine iniquity, and cleanse me from my sin (Psa. 51:1, 2).

He cannot do it. 'Burnt offerings and sacrifices are not enough', he says. He has tried to cleanse his heart, but he knows he cannot do it. His only course, he tells us, is to go back to God himself.

This is the testimony of all who have ever known God's blessing.

> Not the labour of my hands
> Can fulfill thy law's demands;
> Could my zeal no respite know,

88

Could my tears forever flow,
All for sin could not atone;
Thou must save, and thou alone.

This is the initial problem. Any person who is once awakened to their position in life and face to face with God becomes alarmed and concerned. They want to be right in the future. But before you come to the future, what about the past? The stain of sin is upon us, and we cannot touch it. We cannot remove it. And yet we can have no relationship with God while it is there. God cannot even look upon sin.

This is the very essence of the Christian message. The answer to the problem is this: 'Then will I sprinkle clean water upon you, and ye shall be clean: from all your filthiness, and from all your idols, will I cleanse you.' This is the paradox of the gospel. It is all there in Psalm 51: David says, 'Against thee, thee only, have I sinned, and done this evil in thy sight', and yet he knows that the only one who can deliver him and put him right is the very God whom he has offended.

We cannot erase these spots; we can do nothing. Sin is upon us and we cannot get rid of what we have done. So what can we do? The astounding thing is that as we are in our predicament and see and feel our hopelessness, it is God himself who speaks to us and announces that he himself is going to wash us. The very God against whom we have sinned and whom we have offended is himself going to cleanse us, purify us and render us fit to stand in his holy presence.

That leads us to the next step: how does he do it? 'Then will I sprinkle clean water upon you, and ye shall be clean.' That was the way in which they did it in the Old Testament. They used to take a heifer and burn it. Then they took the ashes of the heifer and put them in water and mixed it. And people who had sinned, who had touched a dead body or

SAVED BY GRACE ALONE

had done various other things were sprinkled with this water and thereby cleansed. That was the picture, but it was all a foreshadowing of the glorious message of the New Testament.

How does God wash us from the guilt of our sin? The answer comes in this wonderful message: 'God so loved the world, that he gave his only begotten Son, that whosoever believeth in him should not perish, but have everlasting life' (John 3:16). 'No, no,' says the writer of Hebrews 10, 'the blood of bulls and of goats and the ashes of a heifer cannot really do this. That was a temporary expedient, just to cover it for the time being.' So how is it done? There was someone who came into the world and said, 'Lo, I come to do thy will, O God. A body thou hast prepared me.' In order to deal with this terrible, tragic, appalling problem of our guilt and filthiness, God sent his only Son into this world.

The Lord Jesus Christ came into the world specifically for this problem of our guilt. He did not come merely to teach us, though he did teach. He did not come merely to give us an example, though he did that. But if he had stopped at that, he would have condemned us more than we were already condemned.

I cannot come up to my own standard. I cannot satisfy myself. I read the lives of saints and I feel I am a pygmy and am nothing. And then I look at Jesus of Nazareth and he makes me feel utterly and absolutely hopeless. I read his Sermon on the Mount and I say, 'Who can live such a life? Who can ascend to such a height?' It is so exalted. It is all very well to sit back and say, 'What a wonderful life! Now I'm going to follow him. I'm going to go after him and imitate him. I'm going to live like that.' Have you ever tried doing it? Try it—you will find it is utterly impossible. It simply reveals your weakness. He exposes your sin more than ever.

No, he did not come primarily to do those things. The real object of his coming into the world was as it is put in the epistle to the Hebrews: he 'was made a little lower than the angels for the suffering of death' (Heb. 2:9). He came to taste death for everyone. To put it plainly, the problem of the guilt of our sin was so great that the Son of God had to come from heaven.

Had you realized this? Perhaps you had thought, as so many still seem to think in spite of this open Bible, that God forgives sin because he is love; that all you and I have to do is say we are sorry, and, because God is a God of love, he will forgive us our sins. But why then did the Son of God ever come into this world? It was known in the Old Testament that God is a God of love, that he is full of mercy and compassion. A psalmist could say, 'When my father and my mother forsake me, then the LORD will take me up' (Psa. 27:10). The psalmists write about his longsuffering, his patience and compassion, his goodness, his kindness and his mercy. So why did the Son of God leave the courts of heaven and come to earth, and live and die and rise again?

There is only one answer: because it was absolutely essential. The guilt of our sin could not be dealt with except in that way. So he came on earth to deal with this very problem. And he did not help us to solve it merely by living as he lived or teaching as he taught. That leaves us still more sinful.

How did he solve it, then? There is the law of God thundering out its condemnation of sin, demanding that men and women live righteous and holy lives in the presence of God. And Jesus Christ came, in this body which God had prepared for him, and entered the virgin's womb. He took human nature from her, added it to himself and lived here as a man. And he rendered a perfect obedience to that law of God. He satisfied its every demand.

But even that was not enough. That was enough to enable us to say that we have kept the law in him. But still there is the problem of the sins committed, the sins of the past. What can be done about them?

Here we come to the most wonderful and amazing thing of all: he deliberately identified himself with our guilt and our sins. He went to John the Baptist and he said, 'Baptize me.' John said, 'You don't need to be baptized. I need to be baptized of you. Why do you ask me to baptize you?' Jesus said, 'Suffer it to be so now: for thus it becometh us to fulfil all righteousness' (Matt. 3:15). He identified himself with us in sin. He made himself one of us. He took his stand by our side.

But follow on the story and go and look at him in the garden of Gethsemane. There he is, sweating great drops of blood as he says to his Father, 'If it be possible, let this cup pass by.' What is he talking about? He is talking about your sins and mine. That is the cup. He has come on earth to deliver us from the guilt of our sins. There is only one way it can be done: he has got to take them upon himself. He is going to clothe himself, as it were, with our sins. And God is going to punish our sins in the person of his own Son. 'If it be possible,' he says three times, 'let this cup pass by. Nevertheless not my will but thine be done.' He has come to save us, yet he asks at the last moment, as it were, 'Is this the only way? Does it really mean that when you look upon me on that cross, you are going to see not so much me as the sins of humanity, and you're going to hate them and you're going to smite them and thus we'll be separated? Is this the only way?' But it was the only way, so on he went. And there on Calvary God laid on him the iniquity of us all. As Peter puts it, 'Who his own self bare our sins in his own body on the tree' (1 Pet. 2:24). The sins of men and women were put on him. And God punished him. He smote him. 'With his stripes we are healed' (Isa. 53:5). His blood was shed. And it is the shedding of his blood that alone can cleanse us from the guilt and the filthiness and the foulness of our sins.

'Then will I sprinkle you,' says God, 'with clean water.' It is his action. We cannot get rid of our sins. We cannot make atonement. We cannot undo the past. We cannot offer anything to God that is satisfactory. But God can, and he has. The cleansing is in the blood of Christ, which cleanses from all sin, from every stain, defilement and pollution. And so God makes us fit to come into his presence by shedding the blood of his own Son and sprinkling it upon us.

Ezekiel was given a glimpse of it all. God spoke it to him and told him to tell it to the children of Israel. But we have it in all its fullness, no longer in types and shadows. It has been accomplished. That is why, whenever we take the bread and the wine, we are declaring the Lord's death till he comes, because that is the only way whereby we can be forgiven. Jesus himself said, 'The Son of man came not to be ministered unto, but to minister, and to give his life a ransom for many' (Matt. 20:28). The good shepherd laid down his life for the sheep. It is the only way.

And this way is sufficient. That is emphasized in our text in Ezekiel: 'Then will I sprinkle clean water upon you, and ye shall be clean: from all your filthiness, and from all your idols, will I cleanse you.' In Hebrews 10 the author quotes Jeremiah 31: 'This is the covenant that I will make with them after those days, saith the Lord, I will put my laws into their hearts, and in their minds will I write them; *and their sins and iniquities will I remember no more.*'

This is what we must realize and believe. Having laid our sins upon Christ and having punished them there, God has finished with them. He has cast them into his sea of forget-fulness. 'As far as the east is from the west, so far hath he removed our transgressions from us' (Psa. 103:12). They are gone in Christ.

When he was an old man and knew that his death was at hand, the apostle John wrote his first epistle, wanting Christians to know the joy which he knew as an apostle. He wanted them to have fellowship with the Father and with his Son, Jesus Christ. How is it possible? 'Well,' John says, 'you can have fellowship like that with God while you are in this world. You don't have to wait until you are dead and have gone to heaven to have fellowship with God. Our fellowship is with the Father and with his Son, Jesus Christ, and I want you to have it and to share in it.' But how is this to happen? John has already said, 'This then is the message ... that God is light, and in him is no darkness at all.' How can I have fel-lowship with such a being, when I know that the truth about myself is this:

> Oh! how can I, whose native sphere
> Is dark, whose mind is dim,
> Before th' Ineffable appear
> And on my naked spirit bear
> That uncreated beam?

If God is light and in him is no darkness at all, how can I, who am full of darkness, vileness and ugliness, possibly walk with him? But John says, 'If we walk in the light, as he is in the light, we have fellowship one with another, and the blood of Jesus Christ his Son cleanseth us from all sin' (1 John 1:7). As you walk with God through this world you will fall into sin and you will become spotted again. How can the fellowship continue? The answer is that 'the blood of Jesus Christ his Son cleanseth us from all sin'.

As the apostle Paul puts it in 1 Corinthians 6:9, 10: 'Know ye not that the unrighteous shall not inherit the kingdom of God? Be not deceived: neither fornicators, nor idolaters, nor adulterers, nor effeminate, nor abusers of themselves with mankind, nor thieves, nor covetous, nor drunkards, nor revilers, nor extortioners, shall inherit the kingdom of God.' People like that will not have fellowship with God; they will not know his blessing; they will never be in his kingdom. But verse 11 says: 'And such were some of you.' The Corinthians had been guilty of those foul, vile and filthy things. 'Such were some of you: but ye are washed, but ye are sanctified, but ye are justified in the name of the Lord Jesus, and by the Spirit of our God.' God had washed those Corinthians and made them clean. And they were saints in the church of God and were having fellowship with him.

It is only in the blood of Christ that we are washed; it is only there that we can wash our sins away and make our garments clean and bright. It is in him, says Paul, that 'we have redemption through his blood, the forgiveness of sins' (Eph. 1:7). God's way of forgiveness and cleansing from the guilt of sin is in the blood of Christ.

Hebrews 10:19 speaks of 'Having therefore, brethren, boldness to enter into the holiest.' How can I enter into the holiest? How can I have an audience with God? How can I speak to God? How can I pray to God? How can I be blessed of God? There is only one answer:

> … by the blood of Jesus, by a new and living way, which he hath consecrated for us, through the veil, that is to say, his flesh; and having an high priest over the house of God; let us draw near with a true heart in full assurance of faith, having our hearts sprinkled from an evil [accusing] conscience, and our bodies washed with pure water (Heb.10:19-22).

When you pray to God, do you do it like that? Do you enter into the presence of God with boldness? Do you do so in the full assurance of faith? Do you go to him knowing that your sins are forgiven and that you are his child; that he is delighted to receive you? That is full assurance of faith.

'How can I do that?' asks someone. 'When I go on my knees before God, I'm more conscious of my sins and of my sinfulness than at any other time in my life. And I know that I'm a sinner. How can I go with confidence and boldness when I know I've sinned?'

That is the whole question. If you believe this message concerning Jesus Christ and him crucified, you can go in the full assurance of faith, because you say to yourself, 'Though I am a sinner, though I am guilty of sins, Christ has borne their punishment and guilt. He has taken them away and God will remember them no more. I believe this, so by the blood of Christ I go in as I am, trusting to his perfect work and his merit, knowing that God will honour his word and receive me.' That is the full assurance of faith. It is not ignoring your sins; it is facing them. It is confessing them, admitting them, but saying, 'Yes, but Christ has died for them.'

> His blood can make the foulest clean,
> His blood availed for me.

> There is a fountain filled with blood
> Drawn from Immanuel's veins;
> And sinners plunged beneath that flood
> Lose all their guilty stains.

His blood is the only thing that is strong enough and potent enough to take out the stain of sin. But it is enough. It does not matter what you have been. I cannot give you a list that is worse than that which Paul gives in 1 Corinthians 6. Any sin can be blotted out by the blood of Christ if you but believe he died for you.

So do not talk any longer about your sins or about your fitness. All the fitness you require is to feel your need of him. His blood cleanses from all sin and unrighteousness. If you believe that, go in the full assurance and confidence of faith, pleading only the blood of Christ shed for you and for your sins, and God will receive you and will let you know that your sins and iniquities he will remember no more.

When God washes you in the blood of Christ there is no more remembrance of sin. It is gone. Your sins are forgiven in him. So go to God to thank him and to give yourself to him, and to pledge yourself to live only to the praise, glory and honour of the one who has so loved you that at great cost he has ransomed, rescued, redeemed, cleansed you and brought you back to himself, and is now beginning to shower his blessings upon you.

The first question is the guilt of your past sins. And until they are removed, you are out of relationship with God. But in Christ and him crucified you can be reconciled, restored.

> Ransomed, healed, restored, forgiven,
> Who like thee his praise should sing?

7. A New Heart

A new heart also will I give you, and a new spirit will I put within you: and I will take away the stony heart out of your flesh, and I will give you an heart of flesh.

—Ezekiel 36:26

THIS great passage, from verse 16 to the end of the chapter, is a wonderful exposition of the Christian message. Here is man's problem: How can we ever get back to God and to that place in which God can bless us? This was the one need of the children of Israel, away from God in a strange country. How could they get back to that position where God could again smile upon them and bless them? Well, in this great announcement God says, 'I will take you from among the heathen, and gather you out of all countries, and will bring you into your own land. Then will I sprinkle clean water upon you, and ye shall be clean: from all your filthiness, and from all your idols, will I cleanse you. A new heart also will I give you, and a new spirit will I put within you.'

The first great principle we have seen is that it is all of God. This is not a human philosophy. This is not man seeking for God or seeking a way of escape and at last finding it. No, this is an announcement that comes from God.

And the second thing which we must never lose sight of is the order in which these things are put. That can never be

99

SAVED BY GRACE ALONE

emphasized too much. As we have seen, the first thing that is absolutely essential to us is that our sins should be forgiven; that we should be reconciled to God; that our transgressions and iniquities should be blotted out.

Of course, we do not like that. We do not like the doctrine of sin and of the atonement. To the natural man, it all sounds so legalistic. We do not like the idea of the wrath of God and the need of a sacrifice. The whole world rebels against that. We say that we want help from God, but no help will come to anybody from God until you are in a right relationship to God. And there is only one way to be rightly related to God, and that is to be in the Lord Jesus Christ. There is one God and one mediator between God and men, the man Christ Jesus, who gave himself a ransom for all.

Now that is absolutely basic and fundamental, and we cannot go further unless we are agreed about that first point. The first need is to be sprinkled with clean water, to be cleansed from all our filthiness and our idols. In other words, if we have not seen ourselves as vile, foul and hopeless sinners in the sight of God, so desperate that nothing but the death of God's Son on the cross could possibly save us, I say with reverence that God has nothing to say to us. That is the beginning. We start with repentance and an utter, absolute dependence upon Jesus Christ the Son of God and his perfect work. There is no relationship between God and men and women except in and through Jesus Christ and him crucified. Every other supposed relationship is a false one. It is make-believe, a lie. I say so on the authority of this word.

If it were possible for man to know God and to be reconciled to him and blessed by him apart from Jesus Christ, then the death of Christ on the cross is the most colossal waste that the world has ever seen. It should never have happened; it should never have been allowed. But it is a lie. There is only one way to God, and it is in Jesus Christ and him crucified. It is his blood alone that can cleanse us from all sin and all unrighteousness. Nothing else can; thank God that this can.

That comes first; but it does not stop there. He goes on: 'A new heart also'—there is something further, something additional. You cannot but marvel and wonder at the perfection of this plan of salvation as it is unfolded to us. Why is it not enough that we should be forgiven by the blood of Christ? Is not this the obvious answer? If salvation stopped at that, we would always be back in the same old position that we were before. If God had just taken the children of Israel, forgiven them, brought them back into Canaan and left them as they were, they would do it all over again. They would go back into idolatry and would be back in trouble. That is not God's way of salvation.

When God sets out to save us, he does a thorough work. So he does not merely leave it at the first step: forgiveness and reconciliation. No, having done that he comes on to this second step: he proceeds to deal with the thing that originally sent us wrong.

There are the children of Israel, sitting by the waters in the captivity of Babylon. Why did they ever get there? Because they had rebelled against God. So something needs to be done to prevent them from doing that again. God is not going to take all the trouble to bring them back if it is simply going to happen again. No, he is going to establish them, so something further is needed. He is going to put right that thing which is wrong in human nature and which cuts it off from the blessing of God and from the enjoyment of his life. That is what we deal with in this verse. It is the need of a new heart, a new spirit.

What does this term 'heart' mean? In Scripture 'heart' is a term that must always be handled carefully. Generally, as here, it means 'the centre of a man or woman's personality'. We tend to confine the 'heart' to the emotions and the sensibilities. But in Scripture it has a wider connotation and especially means a person's mind, which is, after all, the biggest and the greatest thing in mankind. What finally differentiates mankind from the animals is the mind, which is a part of God's image in mankind. So the 'heart' stands for a person's mind and understanding.

Then what does it mean by 'spirit'? 'Spirit' of course means 'attitude', but it also means 'motives', our motivation, our reason for doing things, the kind of force that leads us to our decisions.

With the announcement in this verse we are again at one of those vital points which determine our whole outlook. We cannot handle anything more important or more serious than this. I imagine that everybody—even the most flippant and superficial—would grant that we are in trouble and that there is something wrong with the world. But the great question is, what is the matter? What is our trouble? What is our need? What needs to be done in order that we can be put right and can enjoy life under the hand and blessing of God? There are two main views confronting us today with regard to ourselves and our needs.

It is over the very doctrine in this verse that the great divide comes. The popular, non-biblical view says that we are fundamentally and essentially good, but our real trouble is due to the fact that we do not live up to what we are and know we ought to be. The key statement there is that we are fundamentally, and in and of ourselves, essentially good. Therefore, what we need in our failure and misery is instruction. We need teaching, encouragement, help and examples. The basis of our lives, they say, is all right; it is in the superstructure that we go all wrong.

So attention is paid to giving men and women knowledge and information. Improving mankind is the whole rationale of the non-Christian view of life and has been the controlling theory for over a hundred years. According to this view, we do not need to be changed; we need to be made better. And it can be done, they say, through housing and environment. It is impossible, they say, for anybody to live a good life in bad circumstances and surroundings. They do not seem to have read the histories which show us that glorious saints have lived in slums! They simply take it for granted and say that it cannot happen. Bad surroundings make bad people. Good surroundings make good people: so the solution is slum clearance.

Do not misunderstand me. Politically, we all must believe in slum clearance. But do we really believe that by putting people in new houses we will make new people of them? Yet that is the idea. And so the problem is looked at socially, economically, educationally, culturally, and so on, so that in these various ways we can improve mankind. But fundamentally, mankind is all right.

But over and against that comes the biblical view, which is stated so clearly in our text. To put it bluntly, it says that we are radically, basically, foundationally and fundamentally wrong; our trouble is not in the superstructure but in the very foundation itself. Our trouble is not that we are wrong in certain respects, but that we ourselves are wrong: in our hearts, in the very centre of our being, in the very core of our personalities. Therefore, what we need above everything else is not instruction, information, example, encouragement or a kind of 'fill up' to our good efforts, but a new nature, a new heart, a new spirit.

Here is a dividing line; it is a complete watershed. You are in either one or the other of these two positions; you cannot hold both at the same time. Here we are face to face with the great central controlling biblical doctrine which sometimes goes by the name of 'rebirth', 'regeneration' or 'new creation'. Those are the terms that are used everywhere in the Scriptures.

Therefore the whole question before us at this moment is this: What is my view of mankind? Are we creatures who are so fallen and lost that we cannot be improved, or are we those who can be improved? Are we so hopeless that nothing will suit us but to be born again, to be regenerated, to be created anew? You see how obviously vital this question is.

How can we settle which of the two views is right? We have simply to follow what we are told in our text. What is our need? It is that we have a stony heart: 'I will take away the stony heart out of your flesh, and I will give you an heart of flesh.' According to the Scripture, we are wrong in our heart and our spirit. The diagnosis of our heart is that it is a stony heart, which means it is a hard heart. It is obdurate.

This is something that is taught very frequently in the Scriptures. The author of Hebrews says, 'Harden not your hearts' (Heb. 3:8). Do not harden your hearts as those children of Israel did in the provocation in the wilderness. God had brought the children of Israel out of the bondage and captivity of Egypt in a wonderful way. He was leading them towards the promised land of Canaan, and yet of that generation that came out of Egypt, practically none of them entered Canaan. What was the matter? They were all destroyed in the wilderness. They never entered the promised land. Why? It was because they hardened their hearts; they became obdurate with respect to God; they were no longer sensitive to God, his ways and his will.

The writer to the Hebrews puts it another way: they had, he says, 'an evil heart of unbelief' (Heb. 3:12). Again, he puts it like this: 'lest any of you be hardened through the deceitfulness of sin' (3:13). In other words, it is sin that hardens our hearts, making them unresponsive and impervious to truth.

This is clearly of vital concern to us all. The devil comes and tempts us, just as he did at the very beginning in the garden of Eden. He always tries to put something between us and God. Man and woman had been made by God and there they were in the garden, listening to God, waiting for his voice, expecting his message day by day. But the devil came with his suggestion, just to put something between them and God and to undermine their reliance upon God, and to ask questions so that when God's word came there would be a query. That is the beginning of hardening, the deceitfulness of sin which claims to be there to help us and benefit us. It tells us, 'Turn away from God; listen to me', and so we become hardened in our hearts.

As we saw, the word 'heart' is something that applies chiefly to the mind and the will. And here we have a very profound bit of what we may call biblical psychology. It means that as a result of sin, we are in a condition in which the very truth of God can make no impression upon us. It cannot find a place of entry.

Our blessed Lord put this quite perfectly in the parable of the sower. 'A sower went forth to sow,' he said, 'and ... some seeds fell by the way side, and the fowls came and devoured them up' (Matt. 13:3, 4). Why? What happened? The wayside had been so trodden by people that it had become hard. As the sower sowed the seed, it just rested there on the hard surface, and the birds saw it, pounced upon it and took it all away. The result was exactly the same as if the sower had

SAVED BY GRACE ALONE

never been sowing it at all. Our Lord expounds it in these words: 'When any one heareth the word of the kingdom, and understandeth it not'—that is how he interprets it—'then cometh the wicked one, and catcheth away that which was sown in his heart' (13:19). What a perfect exposition of our text! 'When any one heareth the word of the kingdom, and understandeth it not'—that is what the hardening leads to. The word comes, but it means nothing. It does not enter; it does not find a lodging place. It is like that seed falling onto a pavement or onto the stone. There it stays. If you leave it there a century, it will be no deeper. It just remains, but the birds see it—the devil comes and snatches the word away. And it is exactly as if such a person had never heard God's word or the gospel at all.

In 1 Corinthians 2:14 the apostle Paul puts it like this: 'the natural man receiveth not the things of the Spirit of God: for they are foolishness unto him: neither can he know them, because they are spiritually discerned.' There is a natural man sitting and listening to this word of gospel, of life and salvation. He does not receive it; it does not enter into him; it does not get at his heart. Why? Because there is this hardness, this callosity, this obduracy. The word comes, it strikes, it bounces back and it is gone. That is how Paul describes the natural man, and how true it is.

He has already said the same thing earlier in that chapter. He says that when the Lord Jesus Christ was in this world, 'the princes of this world' did not know him: 'for had they known [him], they would not have crucified the Lord of glory' (1 Cor. 2:8). And when he says 'princes', he does not mean only kings and monarchs, he means the great men, the mighty philosophers, the intellectualists, the men who were truly princes in a natural sense. They did not receive him. They rejected him and despised him. They never realized who he was, though he stood in their presence and spoke to them. Why? The only answer is, to use another statement of the apostle, because they were 'dead in trespasses and sins' (Eph. 2:1).

What does all this mean in actual practice? Let me put it in this form: the man who has a hard heart is a man who is dead to everything spiritual. Spiritual things, as the apostle puts it, mean nothing at all to him. God is there in the heavens in eternity, looking upon the earth. He has made the earth and he controls it. He sends the seasons: spring, summer, autumn, winter. He sends a day of glorious sunshine. But these people see nothing at all. They never see God. They do not stop to think at a deep level. They just take it as it comes and curse if it is raining. They do not see God in all the marvel and the glory of it all. They are absolutely dead to God.

Now compare such a man with one of the saints. Read the biography of a saint over against the biography of a man who did not believe in God and had a hard heart. You will find that the saint's life is a romance because he is in relationship to God and God does amazing things with him. He does not know what is going to happen next. He is alive and alert to God. His whole life is centred upon God. Read about a man like Abraham, Moses or David. For all these men, you will find that their life is centred on God. They are alive, alert, responsive. But this other man is absolutely dead to God. He does not believe in God, or if he does, he never thinks about him. He lives his life entirely apart from God, as if there were no God. God does not touch him at all; there is no imprint made upon his life. He is dead to God because of his hard heart.

But they are not only dead to the being of God; they are dead to the fact of their own souls. They never stop to consider and realize that they have a priceless possession within them. They spend the whole of their time thinking of themselves in terms of this life and this world only. They have never even said with Longfellow,

> Dust thou art, to dust returnest,
> Was not spoken of the soul.

That is true of the body, but it was never true of the soul. There is that within men and women which is bigger than their bodies, than their surroundings, than the world; it defies everything, and even though you kill their bodies, it goes on. But these people are oblivious of this. They are not aware of it, or even interested in it. They think only in terms of the body: food, drink, clothing, appearance, and so on—life in this limited little span. Dead to their own souls, they never meditate upon this gigantic thing that is there within them. That is because they have hard hearts.

The Bible is always speaking about these things. It tells men and women about their own greatness. It tells them about their own destiny. It tells them what they were meant to be, what they might be. But it means nothing to them; it bounces back off them. When they hear it, they say, 'That's a waste of time. I'm not interested in it.'

But equally they are dead to their own destiny because it is a sign of spiritual life that a person should be interested in his or her destiny. The man who has a hard heart never sits down and says to himself, 'Where am I going? What will happen when I die? What lies beyond?' That is a spiritual question at once. A man who is concerned about that is spiritually alive, but the man who has a hard heart is not interested in that. He is not interested in the fact that death is not the end and that beyond death you face God and the judgment, and there you are made to listen to the promulgation of a sentence which tells you about your eternal destiny.

The Bible tells us that God is the judge of the whole earth and that he will judge the world in righteousness by that man whom he has appointed, namely his own Son, the Lord Jesus Christ. But say that to a man who has a hard heart and it does not touch him. It makes no impression on him at all. Instead he says, 'Oh, I'm not to be frightened by that sort of thing. You are a hundred years out of date. We know too much to believe that sort of thing now.' It just bounces back. Why? He does not realize, but it is because his heart is hard. He is like that stony ground, that pathway by the side. There is no soil for the seed to go in.

These are some of the consequences of having a stony heart. But there are others, which are more serious and more tragic. People with stony hearts see nothing in the Lord Jesus Christ. If ever they mention his name, it is only as an expletive, a curse, an oath, as something foul, vicious and vile. They have never contemplated his surpassing glory. They have never said, 'Thou art the Lily of the Valley, the Bright and Morning Star, the fairest of ten thousand to my soul.' They do not understand what it was that moved Handel as he composed his *Messiah*. They do not understand the writers of those hymns that say, 'Thou, O Christ, art all I want'; or

> Jesus, the very thought of thee
> With sweetness fills my breast.

It is because their hearts are hard.

Some people can sit and look at the most moving drama that pulls and tugs at your heartstrings, but they are left unmoved and untouched. There are people who can listen to the most glorious oratorios and they are bored. There are people who can read the most sublime poetry and see nothing in it. There are people who can stand and look at an amazing sunset and be interested in something that is on the ground. The trouble with such people is that they have no appreciation. They do not have anything within them that responds. Their hearts are not hearts of flesh; they are hearts of stone, and there is no response. Oh, such people know nothing about the grace of the Lord Jesus Christ in redemption, and all the exceeding riches of his grace and all the wondrous things that are held out to the children of God! They mean nothing to them. Their spiritual life as a whole leaves them absolutely dead and untouched.

And, of course, their spirit—that means, their motive or attitude—is in the same condition. Not only are they failing to appreciate it, but they are even antagonistic. We saw how Paul put it in 1 Corinthians 2:14: 'The natural man,' he says, 'receiveth not the things of the Spirit of God.' But why not? Because 'they are foolishness unto him'. That is antagonism. 'The natural, or carnal, mind,' says the apostle again, in Romans 8:7, 'is enmity against God.' It is a hatred of God and nothing less than that. You see, it does not stop at merely a lack of response; there is a positive opposition, a definite antagonism.

John puts it like this: 'This is the condemnation, that light is come into the world' (John 3:19). Why does everybody not believe in it and bask in it? 'Men loved darkness rather than light, because their deeds were evil.' Why is there a hatred of it? Because that which makes manifest is light, and when the light comes it exposes the hidden things of darkness, and people do not like that. So they hate the light. They say, 'If that light comes I shan't be able to go on doing these things. Therefore, put out the light.'

It is like those men in Gadara after our blessed Lord had driven the devils out of the poor possessed lunatic man and he was seated, clothed and in his right mind. Instead of thanking him, they besought him to depart out of their coasts. Why? It was because he had driven the devils into the swine, and the swine had hurtled themselves to destruction, down in the depths of the sea. They said, 'If this man stays here, he's going to ruin our trade. He's making things impossible. Therefore, get rid of him.' Get rid of the light in order that you may go on enjoying the hidden things of darkness. Man's spirit is wrong as well as his heart.

Is there anything that can be more hopeless than this? Is it really just enough to teach such a man? Our Lord himself has said that it is not. Is there any point in going on sowing seed onto this path by the side of the field where there is no possibility of its going in and producing anything, where the birds go at once and take it? Why, you are simply wasting seed! Nothing can be done for such a person. Is teaching alone going to do it? Is appealing alone going to do it? What is the use of appealing, even with the greatest tenderness imaginable, to a man or woman who hates God and who regards God and all that belongs to him as foolishness?

The Scripture is right: what such a person needs is a new heart, a new spirit. Do what you like to that person, it will never avail. You cannot get a crop off a pathway; you need new soil. You need a new heart, a new spirit, a new everything. And that is the very thing that is promised and offered in this blessed and glorious gospel: a change of heart, a change of spirit.

The New Testament speaks of it in terms of rebirth, regeneration, new life, the dead receiving a new heart, a new creation. Had you realized that this is the gospel? The gospel of

Jesus Christ is a miracle. It does not improve people; it makes them anew. It gives us a new heart and a new spirit.

And what is emphasized so plainly in our text and in all the context is that this is God's action. No one can make a Christian but God. A man cannot make himself a new heart or change his own spirit. 'Can the Ethiopian change his skin, or the leopard his spots?' (Jer. 13:23). That is as easy as some-one giving themselves a new heart. Have you ever tried to give yourself a new heart? Have you ever tried to be interested in the Bible? Have you ever tried to make yourself a new person? If you have, you know it cannot be done.

But thank God, we are not asked to do it. It is God who says, 'A new heart also will I give you, and a new spirit will I put within you: and I will take away the stony heart out of your flesh, and I will give you an heart of flesh.' It is God alone who can work miracles. We cannot do it. But God works this miracle of redemption: 'a heart of flesh'. And what does this mean? It is the exact opposite of all I have been saying. God in Christ offers to put a new principle into your life, something that was not there before, something that makes you therefore entirely different.

What is this new principle of life? Essentially it is this. To start with the mind, it is a new ability to see and to appre-hend truth. These new people say, 'You know, what I cannot understand is this: how could I have missed it? How could I have failed to see it? It's so plain. It's there everywhere.' Some-times, having been converted and having had this new heart with this new principle of life and this new understanding, they are of course very anxious that those who are nearest and dearest to them should have it also; and they become a little impatient with them. 'But,' they say, 'they can't see it, and it's so obvious!'

This simply emphasizes what a miracle it is, that this new principle makes the thing so plain and clear that one simply cannot believe afterwards that one was ever blind to it! And yet we were all like that by nature.

When the new principle is given, when the new heart is put in, we begin to see things. The Bible is so clear. It is such an interesting, exciting, romantic book. And here is truth, this marvellous truth about God and creation, and men and women and what they are, and I myself and my soul, my sinfulness, Christ as my redeemer, my new relationship to him, and so on.

The testimony of every person who has received a new heart is this: 'whereas I was once blind, now I see.' They are in a new world. They feel that they are new people altogether. They have an entirely new outlook and understanding. The things they previously lived for, they now see as a waste of time. And the things they dismissed as foolishness and boredom are the only things that matter to them. They have a new mind.

Here is Paul again in 1 Corinthians: 'The princes of this world knew [him not]: for had they known [him], they would not have crucified the Lord of glory ... But God hath revealed [these things] unto us by his Spirit: for the Spirit searcheth all things, yea the deep things of God.' God, he goes on to say, has not given us the spirit that is of the world, 'but the spirit which is of God; that we might know the things that are freely given to us of God' (1 Cor. 2:8, 10, 12). We come to this knowledge. We have the mind of Christ.

And, of course, in the same way the spirit is changed. This man is no longer antagonistic to God. What he desires above everything else is God. I testify to that; it is nothing in me, but I say to the glory of God and in order to be honest that there is nothing in heaven or earth or sea or under the sea that I desire beyond God. To know God is my supreme delight, my chiefest desire.

> I was not ever thus, nor prayed that thou
> Shouldst lead me on.

But now there has been a change, there is a difference; for the hymnwriter adds,

> I loved to choose and see my path; *but now*
> Lead thou me on.

There is a new spirit, a delight in these things, a desire for God, the living God. 'As the hart panteth after the water brooks, so panteth my soul after thee, O God' (Psa. 42:1). That is how the new man speaks. He loves God. He desires to know God's will and to do it. He desires to glorify God. It is the exact opposite of the other picture that I painted.

What a glorious gospel this is! Because this is God's work, it is possible for all. And that is what, if I may so put it, makes preaching the gospel such a romance. I know that there is no one who is so hopeless but that God can change them. I cannot; no one can. Education and culture cannot. They have all failed so often. But I know that if there is someone who has touched rock bottom and whose heart is as hard and as obdurate as a stone, God can melt it and take it out of them and put in a heart of flesh.

Thank God that the vilest blasphemer and rejecter of God and of Christ has as much a chance of becoming a saint as the most respectable person in the land, because it is God's work, because it is a miracle, because it is the power of God unto salvation, and he is able to do it. He has been doing it down the running centuries. He is still doing it. He will go on doing it until the number of the elect is complete.

My final question is this: has it happened to you? The Lord
Jesus Christ and his abasement, his death upon the cross: does
it mean anything to you, or does it just strike your heart as the
seed struck the wayside? Does it just fall on you and bounce
off, and you do not want to hear it again and you see nothing
in it?

If that is the case, it is because your heart is hard. It is
stony. It is like that wayside that never bears a crop. It is so
unlike that field over there with a glorious crop—thirtyfold,
sixtyfold, some a hundredfold.

Is your heart hard or have you got this heart of flesh? What
is your spirit like? Is it antagonistic to God and these things,
or have you got a hunger for them, a thirst for them, a desire
to know them? You will never have a more important question put to you than that; the writer to the Hebrews says that
the people with a hard heart, the evil heart of unbelief, who
did not receive the word mixed with faith perished in the
wilderness and their carcasses were seen (Heb. 3). Terrible
though it is to contemplate, whoever dies with a hard and
stony heart has nothing to look forward to but perishing. God
forbid that anybody today hearing this gospel, which offers a
new heart and a new spirit, a heart of flesh, sensitive and alive
to God and all his gifts and glories, should be unaffected by it.
I tremble as I think of it, but I am afraid that to such a soul in
an eternity of torment, even my feeble words will come back
as condemnation. God forbid it! And therefore, if you feel
that you are hard and that your spirit is obdurate, oh, let me
plead with you: cry out to him and say with David, 'Create
in me a clean heart, O God; and renew a right spirit within
me' (Psa. 51:10). If you want it, he will give it to you. Do not
be made to feel hopeless by Satan. Do not say, 'I'm hopeless.
I feel nothing.' The question is: do you want a new heart? If

you do, there is everlasting hope. Cry out to him, and he will take out of you the heart of stone and in its place put in a heart of flesh, and you will be a new person in Christ Jesus.

8. I Will Put My Spirit Within You

*And I will put my spirit within you, and cause you to walk
in my statutes, and ye shall keep my judgments, and do them.*
—Ezekiel 36:27

IT increasingly seems to me that men and women who do
not enjoy the blessings of Christian salvation are in that
condition because they have never truly realized what the
gospel is and especially what it has to offer. We all tend to
think that we know what the gospel is, but for that reason
people have never really faced it. So I am calling attention to
this particular verse and to the surrounding context because
here we have a perfect declaration of the gospel of our Lord
and Saviour Jesus Christ.

As one has the privilege of talking to people about these
things here and elsewhere, one is constantly discovering that
there is a basic misconception, some failure to understand or
to grasp one of the very first principles of the gospel of Christ.
There is only one explanation of all this, of course: it is the
work of the adversary of God and of the souls of men, the
devil. Insinuating a false idea of Christianity into our minds,
in a sense he never allows us, as best he can, to face what is
actually the truth.

As we look at this description of the gospel, I think that
point becomes abundantly clearer. Now, no failure on the part

of men and women with respect to the gospel is perhaps quite as great as the failure to grasp the completeness of the gospel. All along we tend to stop at certain points. And because we stop at those points, we not only never have an adequate conception of the gospel as it is itself, but to that extent also we fail to reap the benefits which it can give us.

As we go on, therefore, from step to step in this picture we have here of the gospel, that point comes out very clearly. Notice that the statement is put in general that what Christianity offers to do is to deliver us out of a captivity. It is something that will take hold of us and bring us out from amongst the heathen and bring us back to the place where God intended us to be and where God will bless us. That is really the whole purpose of this Christian message. It is not just a call or an invitation to us to do certain things; long before it comes to that, it first of all announces what God is going to do to us. We need to be delivered, set free. And that is what the gospel does.

It then goes on to tell us how this happens. We have seen the importance of taking these things in the order in which they are given here, which is exactly the order in which they are given in the New Testament. And we have seen that the first thing we all need in this life and in this world is forgiveness: to be cleansed from our sin and from the guilt of our sin. The gospel offers to do that through Jesus Christ and him crucified.

But then we have also seen that we need a new kind of faculty. Why is man in misery and wretchedness? Why does he sin? Why does he ever need forgiveness? The problem is that man has a mind and a heart that are alienated from God. And so we need a new nature, a new heart, a new understanding. We have seen that God also promises to give us that. He is going to take out this stony, obdurate heart that is impervious

to truth, and give us a heart that can understand and compre-
hend.

But even that is not all. And it is here we begin to see
more clearly the comprehensive character of this salvation. It
does not stop there, and that is because, in and of itself, that
is really not enough. We can see that our sins are forgiven
because Jesus Christ has borne them in his own body on the
tree and has suffered their penalty, and thereby we are washed
in the blood of Christ and our sins have been removed. We are
reconciled to God through Jesus Christ who has been made
sin for us. This, though, leaves us with a problem. How are
we to live this Christian life?

God says he is going to bring these people back from Babylon and their captivity, back to their own land. But what is the
point of doing that if they are just the same as they were before?
It was in that land that they went wrong, that they sinned and
turned their backs upon God. Will they not do the same again?
It is all very well to be brought back to Canaan, but how are
we going to live a godly life there? How can we keep God's
commandments? How can we honour his judgments?

That is the next problem which confronts us. And I think
this is a point at which many people stumble as they consider
this gospel; it is this whole problem of the need of power,
of strength and help. How often people listen to the gospel
and say, 'Oh, that's wonderful! I can see that my past can be
forgotten, that my sins are blotted out. I see this new understanding, this new insight into truth. And I am on the verge
of giving into it and yielding to it—but how can I live the life?
I feel the power of it when I'm listening to it in chapel, or as
I read it at certain times. And I want to give myself to it. I'd
like to be like that. But I know that the whole thing is futile,
because I'm still the same person, and I've got to go back out

into the same world. The world and the flesh and the devil don't change and I know that my own nature is weak. How often I have wished that I could live a better life! How often I have tried to do so, and I've really meant it! I've taken my resolutions. I've made my vows. I've promised others. I've done my utmost, but I have failed, and failed miserably. So what can I do about it? It is all very well to talk about being put back into Canaan. But what guarantee have I that I am going to be different from what I was before? How can I obey God and live this godly life?'

Many have stumbled at that. They say that they do not want to make fools of themselves. They are afraid of being carried away by the moment. But what such people have never realized is what we are told in this verse, Ezekiel 36:27. Having done the other things, God says, 'And I will put my spirit within you, and cause you to walk in my statutes, and ye shall keep my judgments, and do them.'

I must emphasize again a principle which has been recurring right through our consideration of this passage: it is still God's action. Notice this blessed 'I'. I think that men and women forget that salvation is God's work from the very beginning to the very end. The gospel of Jesus Christ does not ask you to make yourself a Christian. It does not ask you to change your life; it knows you cannot. It knows that you can make some superficial reformation but that you cannot change your nature.

No, it is God who is going to do all these things, and God is going to do this further thing. What is it? This is the promise of the Holy Spirit, and there is nothing more wonderful about the gospel than this. Indeed, in many ways it is the very essence of this Christian message. Here Ezekiel looks forward to the day of Pentecost and to the wonderful things that happened when the ascended glorified Son of God sent down and poured forth his Holy Spirit upon the church. That is a part of this gospel of salvation, this message of redemption. God is going to do this further thing.

It is vital to grasp this. If you read the Acts of the Apostles, you simply cannot understand it apart from this particular promise. Look at people like the apostle Peter and others whom we read about in the Gospels, who cut such a sorry figure and who were such miserable failures. When Peter was challenged as to whether he belonged to Jesus Christ, he said, 'I don't know the man', and three times he denied him with oaths and cursing. He did it all simply to save his own skin because he was a coward, afraid of death. Look at all those disciples fumbling and stumbling. Our Lord speaks to them about his death and resurrection, and they cannot grasp it and object to it. What fools they seem to be!

But then look at them in the Acts of the Apostles. How entirely different they are! What a boldness appears in Peter! What an understanding of the Scriptures; what an ability to preach! 'These men,' says someone, 'have turned the world upside' (Acts 17:6). But they were just ordinary fishermen, ignorant men in a sense, and yet they were able to work miracles and do marvellous things. How was that? The answer is that God had fulfilled what he had prophesied here through Ezekiel: 'I will put my spirit within you.' The Acts of the Apostles is really the book of the Acts of the Holy Ghost in and through the apostles. It was this energy, this power, this divine strength that came upon them.

Indeed, you cannot understand the story of the Christian church throughout the centuries apart from this. This power has gone into pagan lands and has revolutionized the lives of people: cannibals becoming saints, men and women, sitting in the darkness, in the squalor and filth of sin, becoming noble citizens. What is it? Is it merely education? If it is, why does it not do the same thing in this country? Is it the mere exhortations of men? If it is, why does it not do the same thing everywhere? No, there is only one answer: it is this power of the Holy Spirit, this energy of God.

It is therefore absolutely vital that we should understand it. And that is true not only in general, in the whole history of the church, but also in the life of a single individual Christian. Christianity is the most revolutionary force that this world has ever known. This is something that really does so change men and women that not only do other people have difficulty in recognizing them to be the same, but the Christians find it extremely difficult to recognize themselves. There is no more perfect statement of Christianity than that of Paul in Galatians 2:20: 'I live; yet not I, but Christ liveth in me.' 'I am myself; I'm not myself. I am Saul of Tarsus, but patently I'm not; I'm the apostle Paul. I'm a new man; I'm a new creation.' This is the power of the Holy Spirit.

Go through the book of Acts again. Look at Saul of Tarsus. Look at his conversion in chapter 9. Look at the Philippian jailer: on the verge of committing suicide in desperation, the next moment rejoicing in God with all his house. Go through and read the biographies of the saints of the centuries; read about the able philosopher and yet dissolute immoral man Augustine of Hippo. I see him now a doctor of the church, a great saint. What has happened to him? Has he got a new philosophy? No, it is a power that has entered his life: the power of this Holy Spirit.

This is a vital part of Christianity. Christianity is not just a little moral teaching or a new ideology. People cannot be changed fundamentally by ideas. They can change their ideas, and up to a point that will affect their lives; but that is not the gospel. The gospel is the Holy Spirit being put into us by God himself. It is something absolutely different.

Have you realized how central this is? Are you doubtful and hesitant about Christianity? Are you afraid of some future failure? Are you saying, 'What's the use of giving myself if I know I am going to fail tomorrow because of what I am and because the world is what it is?' The answer is, 'I will put my spirit,'—*my spirit,*—'within you.' That is the gospel of the Spirit sent by Christ to those for whom he died and to whom he has given the new mind, understanding and enlightenment.

What does 'my spirit' mean? This is the great doctrine of the Holy Spirit. The Holy Spirit is none other than the third person in the blessed holy Trinity: God the Holy Spirit. There is one God in three persons, God the Father, God the Son and God the Holy Ghost. Do not try to understand this; I do not understand it. And God says, 'I will put him, my Spirit, within you.' The Holy Spirit comes to dwell within believers in the Lord Jesus Christ and revolutionizes their lives; nothing less than that. John Wesley, no mean judge in these matters, used to say that his favourite definition of Christianity was this title of a book by a man called Henry Scougal, a Scotsman who had lived towards the end of the seventeenth century: *The Life of God in the Soul of Man.* That is Christianity.

Be clear, then, about the person of the Holy Spirit. The Holy Spirit is not just an influence or a power. The Holy Spirit is a person, as much a person as the Lord Jesus Christ was, as much as God the Father is. And here is the wonderful thing: the Holy Spirit, the third person, is going to take up his tabernacle within us and dwell in our very bodies. It is a great and extensive doctrine.

We cannot go into that doctrine now, but I want to empha-size one aspect: the power of the Godhead, the power of the Holy Spirit that has been doing the things that I have been describing. It is all there in the book of Acts, and it is every-where in the history of the church. His power is invincible, irresistible. There is no limit to what he can do; and God puts this Spirit, this person with this power, within our lives and so enables us to keep his commandments and to carry out his judgments.

How does he do this? There are many answers to that ques-tion in the New Testament. It is all in Philippians 2:12, 13: 'work out your own salvation with fear and trembling. For it is God which worketh in you both to will and to do of his good pleasure.'

Let us interpret this in the light of that statement. The ques-tion is: how am I to live this godly life? The answer is—if I can put it like this in a preliminary manner—that God the Holy Spirit works within you. I know nothing about the gospel that is more wonderful than this. You are not left to yourself. God does not just forgive you and give you a new insight and understanding, and then leave you to yourself to battle it all out. No, he puts his Spirit within you. You are not abandoned in this struggle against sin. He comes to you; he takes up his abode in you. And his energy, might and power begin to work within you.

Just before his death, our Lord offered up a great prayer known as the high-priestly prayer, which we find in John 17. There, amongst other things, he offered this petition: '[Father], sanctify them through thy truth: thy word is truth' (verse 17). The Lord Jesus Christ is about to be crucified, to die and to rise again and go back to heaven. And he is leav-ing this handful of followers: simple, ignorant, fallible, frail men, men whom Satan had defeated and had got down, and who, as I said, had failed in so many respects. Christ's whole honour is in their hands. He says, 'I am glorified in them.' He is leaving them in this great world opposed to him, so opposed to him that it crucified him, to face the devil and hell. What chance do they stand? But he prays for them, 'Sanctify them through thy truth: thy word is truth.' He had already told them that if he went, after he had gone he would send his Spirit upon them. Well here it is: the Spirit and the word; and God answered the prayer by sending the Holy Spirit upon them. And he works in us in order to produce the desired end.

Notice that this is still the action of God. Just as God says, 'Then will I sprinkle clean water upon you' and 'A new heart also will I give you, and a new spirit will I put within you: and I will take away the stony heart out of your flesh, and I will give you an heart of flesh,' so he also says, 'And I will put my spirit within you.' Notice how definite and certain it is: 'And I will … cause you to walk in my statutes, and ye shall keep my judgments, and do them.'

People have often been confused over this. There are some people who seem to think and to teach, alas, that you can accept your forgiveness and your justification from God and decide either to accept or refuse this further offer of sanctification. To me that is a denial not only of this verse but of the whole teaching of the New Testament on this subject of sanctification. There is no gap between justification and sanctification. The God who is going to wash me is the God who puts his Spirit within me. It is all his action. You cannot be a Christian who is just forgiven and no more; there is no such thing. The process is one. There are steps and stages, and it is God who takes the first step, the second step and the third; it

is he who manipulates it all. 'Work out your own salvation ...
It is God which worketh in you.'

I am emphasizing this because it would be inconsistent in
God just to redeem us, to rescue us , to reconcile us to himself
and then to leave us as we were. Why did God send his Son
into this world to die for sinners? Do you think it can possibly
stop at forgiveness and leave us as we were? That is unworthy
of God! What a vast, grand concept this salvation is! From
beginning to end, can God leave it like that? It is impossible,
and indeed he says specifically that he is not going to leave
it at that. God is not going to put us back there and leave us
as we were. No, he is going to make certain that we keep his
commandments: 'I will do this.'

Why did Christ die? Was it merely that you and I might be
forgiven? The New Testament does not say that. Instead it
says this: 'Who gave himself for us, that he might ... purify
unto himself a peculiar people, zealous of good works' (Titus
2:14). Thank God that he died that we might be forgiven,
but it does not stop there: he died to make us good. Can he
possibly leave the job half finished? That is an insult to God.
No, when God starts this process of salvation, he goes on with
it. He cannot leave us simply justified alone. The moment we
are justified and born again, this other process has already
started. And the giving of the Spirit guarantees it.

I want to make this very plain and clear because to me it
is a vital matter. I read an article the other day written by
Charles G. Finney in 1840 in the *Oberlin Evangelist*. You may
have read of Finney and of the revivals that took place under
his ministry in America in the nineteenth century. Thousands
of people were converted under his ministry. But by this point
Finney had ceased to be an evangelist and he was teaching in a
college, and looking back, he said, 'Most of these converts of

mine are a disgrace to Christianity. If I had my time over again as an evangelist, I'd preach nothing but holiness.'

Let us be clear about this. The apostle John says: 'If we say that we have fellowship with him, and walk in darkness, we lie, and do not the truth' (1 John 1:6). 'If we say that we have fellowship with him'—by which we mean that we believe that Christ has died for us to reconcile us to God. Do you say that? Do you believe that Christ died for you? Do you say that you have fellowship with God in Jesus Christ and him crucified? If you do, says John, and yet walk in darkness and go on living in darkness, you lie and do not the truth.

But in the second chapter of that first epistle John goes further: 'He that saith, I know him [God], and keepeth not his commandments, is a liar, and the truth is not in him' (2:4). This is a very serious thing. If you say that you are a Christian because Christ has died for you and you are still living the life of sin, you are a liar, says John. That is his language, not mine. 'But whoso keepeth his word, in him verily is the love of God perfected: hereby know we that we are in him' (verse 5).

So if you claim to be in Christ and believe that Christ has purchased your redemption and has reconciled you to God, and you are rejoicing that you are in Christ, this is the way to know it: because you are keeping the commandments of God. You cannot separate these things. You cannot stop at forgiveness. You cannot stop at the rebirth. You must go on to this, the giving of the Spirit who enables us by his power.

How, then, does he do this? 'It is God which worketh in you', says Paul. How does he do the work? Paul answers the question: he 'worketh in you both to will and to do'. Both these things are necessary in us because, as we are by nature, we do not will these things. We do not want them. We have a carnal mind and our wills are opposed to the will of God.

The natural mind is enmity against God; it is not subject to the law of God. Neither indeed can it be, and that is what we all are by nature. Nobody need deny that; it is a fact. We all of us by nature are rebels against God and our wills are opposed to God. So the first thing I need is for something to be done to my will—and the Holy Spirit does it.

First of all, he shows us sin for what it really is. The prophet Ezekiel puts this very clearly in verse 31 of this chapter: 'Then shall ye remember your own evil ways, and your doings that were not good, and shall lothe yourselves in your own sight for your iniquities and for your abominations.' Of course, while they were doing these things they did not loathe them and they did not loathe themselves. But after the Spirit has come, they look back and say, 'Is it possible that I ever lived like that? Could I ever have sunk to so low a level and have been so vile and so utterly abominable?' That is the work of the Spirit.

It is he alone who can show us sin for what it is, in its vileness, ugliness and foulness. I am thinking not only of drunkenness, adultery and murder, but also of jealousy, envy, spite, malice and ambition, one of the ugliest of all. Oh, what a foul, horrible thing it is—but it takes the Spirit to make us see that. And when he does it, he is already beginning to influence the will. When you see sin's horror, you hate it and you do not want it.

But the Spirit also shows us the beauty of holiness. Oh, what a clean, pure thing it is! I remember how a woman who had once been a paid medium amongst the spiritualists was converted and became a Christian. She explained to me how it had happened. She was prevented in a most extraordinary way from going to a spiritualist meeting where she was to be a medium and to be paid two guineas for doing so. Instead, she had come into a Christian service. She said, 'This was the first thing that happened, and the thing I could never forget again. I came into that meeting and I was conscious that there was a similar power in that chapel as there had been in our spiritualist meetings. But there was this tremendous difference: this power seemed to be clean.' She was conscious not only of power, but of something clean that she had never known before.

There are evil spirits, and they are very powerful. Do not depreciate their might and their strength. But they are vile, ugly, foul spirits. But this spirit is the Holy Spirit, and he gives us a glimpse of the beauty of holiness, the saintly life, the life of Christ himself and of those who followed him most closely. And as the result of this he begins to create a desire within us to be like that and to have that. The holiness which we hated before and laughed at we now desire. Our Lord said, 'Blessed are they which do hunger and thirst after righteousness: for they shall be filled' (Matt. 5:6).

Do you think it is possible that someone who has lived a lifetime steeped in sin and in the gutters of vileness can ever desire and hunger and thirst after holiness and righteousness? It happens. It is precisely what the Holy Spirit does. We ourselves could never do it. But the Holy Spirit can do it and he does it.

But then he goes on and he shows us our own true nature and character. I now see sin in its vileness. I see the beauty of holiness. I want to be like that. 'I'm going to be like that', I say. And then this is what I find, as Paul has described in Romans 7: 'to will is present with me; but how to perform that which is good I find not.' 'With my mind I desire to serve the law of God, but I find another law in my members opposed to the law of my mind. The evil that I would not, that I do. And the

good that I would, I do not. O wretched man that I am!' I am
hopeless—I am two men, I am pulling against myself. It is a
perpetual tug of war. There is a contradiction in my nature, a
horrible dualism in my life. What can I do? It is hopeless! 'O
wretched man that I am! who shall deliver me?' I cannot.

Have you ever come to that? Nothing but the Holy Spirit
makes a man speak like that. A natural man does not speak
like that, does he? He can do anything. He has got it in him to
live a life like Christ. He talks about the imitation of Christ.
He talks about changing his life. He puts himself right with
God. That is a natural man.

But when the Holy Spirit has worked in people, they are
given to see not only the horror of sin and the beauty of holiness, but their own tragic weakness, 'the law in my members'
dragging me down so that I am a mass of contradictions and
am paralysed in failure. That is how he works in me to will.
He creates a longing and a desperation, so that I cry out, 'I
need power! I need strength! I need something within me that
can enable me to do what I want to do and to cease doing
what I hate!'

'It is God which worketh in you both to will and to do.'
This is where the power comes in. 'He breaks the power of
cancelled sin, he sets the prisoner free.' The Holy Spirit, with
his divine might, enables me to mortify the deeds of the body
within me. Though I am forgiven, they are still there. Though
I am regenerate, they still drag me down. It is only the might
and the strength of the Holy Spirit that can enable me to mortify them, to strangle them. 'If ye through the Spirit do mortify
the deeds of the body,' says Paul in Romans 8:13, 'ye shall
live.' Without the power and the strength of the Spirit, no one
can mortify the deeds of the body; it is impossible. But with
the Spirit it becomes possible.

Not only that, he also enables one to live this divine life. He enables one to live the Sermon on the Mount. 'Surely that's impossible!' you say. 'The Sermon on the Mount says, "Love your enemies." Can anyone do that?' No, not in their own strength, but filled with the Spirit they can.

Remember Stephen, a man who was filled with this Holy Spirit. There they are, stoning him. He had done them no wrong; he was simply a Christian, and they stoned him in anger and wrath. And there he is, dying. And what is he doing as he is dying? He is kneeling and praying. This is what he prays: 'Lord, lay not this sin to their charge' (Acts 7:60). He is loving his enemies. The power of the Spirit within him is enabling him to live the life that the Son of God himself lived. He taught us to love our enemies and to do good to them that hate us and to pray for them that use us despitefully and malign us. He enables us; he alone can.

And he will give you spiritual abilities that will amaze you and astound you. Do you know that it takes the power of the Holy Spirit to enable a person to enjoy their Bible? I am not surprised when people say they find the Bible dull and boring. The Bible must be dull and boring to every person who does not have the power of the Spirit within them. It is only the energy of the Spirit that can give you understanding and appreciation.

And what a task is prayer! Have you not almost given up in despair many times when you have tried to pray? It is a task that is impossible to the natural person. But with the energy of the Spirit, one can pray.

I can even put it like this. It is one thing to talk; it is another thing to preach. It is one thing to deliver a sermon; it is another thing to speak in the energy of the Spirit. I can assure you that there is almost an eternity of difference between the two things. He alone can enable one truly to preach the gospel.

The apostle Paul sums it all up in this great phrase: 'I can do all things through Christ which strengtheneth me' (Phil. 4:13). There is one who is 'able to keep you from falling, and to present you faultless before the presence of [God's] glory with exceeding joy' (Jude 24). That is how he does the work: in the will and in the doing. He prepares the mind, he creates the desire, he leads everything to it, and then, after we have seen it, he gives the energy divine, the power, that amazes a man himself. And he asks, 'Is it I? Is it possible?'

He will continue with this work until we are perfect, entire, faultless and blameless, without any spot. 'I will put my spirit within you, and cause you to walk in my statutes, and ye shall keep my judgments, and do them.' 'He which hath begun a good work in you,' says Paul, 'will perform it until the day of Jesus Christ' (Phil. 1:6). To quote Jude again, he is able not only to 'keep you from falling', but also to 'present you faultless'. He will deal with us in his energy until we shall be without spot or wrinkle or any such thing. Listen again to Paul in Ephesians: 'Christ also loved the church, and gave himself for it; that he might sanctify and cleanse it with the washing of water by the word, that he might present it to himself a glorious church, not having spot, or wrinkle, or any such thing; but that it should be holy and without blemish' (5:25-27). That is why he gave himself for the church.

He is going to do it. And—I say it with reverence—he must do it, for in heaven nothing unclean or impure shall enter in. 'Without are dogs, and sorcerers, and whoremongers, and murderers', says Revelation 22:15. How can anybody dwell in the presence of God who has a vestige of impurity? It is impossible. We must be delivered and cleansed from sin. We must be enabled to satisfy God's law on demand, and the Holy Spirit guarantees that. And he will go on with the work within us until we stand before him entire and absolutely perfect.

Is this work going on in you? Are you aware of the working of the Holy Spirit within you? Is he working in your will? Is he disturbing you? Do you still find the commandments of God grievous? Do you feel that the Christian life is horribly narrow? Do you think it would be a terrible thing to spend a week with Jesus Christ because of the way he lived and what he did not do? Is all this revolting to you? Is it harsh and cruel? Is your heart still in the world? Are you loving that kind of life?

If you are, it is no use telling me that Christ died for you. Because the people he died for, he died to separate them from that, and to separate them unto himself, that they might be a holy people. He died not so that they might be forgiven and go on like that. No, he is preparing us for heaven and for glory.

Is this work going on in you? It is a part of the process, whose steps are all interlinked and indivisible. Are you aware of the energy of the Spirit of God within you? You are not redeemed otherwise.

Do you know what it is to be filled with despair about yourself? Are you hungering and thirsting after righteousness? Do you want to be like Christ and to be nearer to him and to know him? Are you looking forward to spending eternity with him? There is no value in believing that you have given yourself to Christ unless there is some evidence of this. There is no separation between justification and sanctification. His commandments are not grievous to those for whom he has died and who belong to him.

Do you know that God has put his Spirit within you? Are you aware of his presence? And are you aware that you are being dealt with and moulded? Are you aware of Another who has come into you and who is drawing you away from the world and drawing you to Christ, and making him increasingly precious in your sight? Do not talk about the blood of Christ unless it has awakened in you longings, aspirations, after holiness and to be like him.

Thank God for such a complete salvation! Thank God that a day is coming when we shall indeed be perfect and stand faultless before the presence of God's glory with exceeding joy. If this is going on within you, God bless you. Yield to him more and more. But if you are doubtful or uncertain, or unhappy, make no tarrying. Go to God and confess it. Acknowledge it. Tell him that you have been making merchandise of the blood of his Son as an excuse for sin. Ask him to send the Spirit and to begin the mighty operation. And give yourself no rest, no peace, until you know that the Spirit of God is in you and that he is working in you mightily, both to will and to do, and, as the result, you are working out your own salvation with fear and trembling.

9. A Great and Complete Salvation

And ye shall dwell in the land that I gave to your fathers; and ye shall be my people, and I will be your God.
—Ezekiel 36:28

HERE is another of those steps which we find recorded here in the blessings of the Christian salvation. I concentrate on the second half of the verse because we have already dealt with the first half in looking at verse 24; it is a repetition of that. But here is the new thing: 'and ye shall be my people, and I will be your God.'

I confess that I find the order in which these things come fascinating. You notice the steps and the stages of salvation, and you must never vary it; you must take them exactly in the order they come. And the interesting thing to notice about this order is that it is the exact reverse of the order in which things happened to man and woman when they fell from God into sin. That is where we see the absolute perfection of God's plan of salvation.

Let us start there with the fall. Of all the terrible things that happened when man and woman sinned and fell, the most terrible was the first thing. God had made them for himself and he had put them in the garden. They dwelt there in a state of fellowship and communion with God. That was their highest privilege, something that they alone enjoyed.

The animals have no fellowship with God; it is only human beings who were made for fellowship with him. God made man and woman in his own image for that reason. And the first thing that went wrong was that they broke that fellowship and that relationship by listening to the talk of Satan, accepting his query about the character and the goodness of God. Everything else followed from that. Because of that, they became unclean. They became opposed to God and his holy laws. Darkness descended upon their minds and they became filthy, foul, sunk into sin and degradation and all the vileness that you can see in the world today.

But they did not suddenly fall from their position as perfect in the presence of God to the squalor, filth and vileness of sin; they went from step to step and stage to stage. But the fatal first thing was the loss of the connection with God. Because of that, all the rest followed, until we see man and woman—ourselves—in a state of filthiness and unclean, bespattered and besmirched in soul by the mud, mire and filth of the world. That is the order.

So when God comes to save us in his one salvation, he does everything, as he must of necessity do, in the reverse order. The object always is to bring us back to where we were. 'I will take you from among the heathen, and gather you out of all countries, and will bring you into your own land.' That is repeated in our verse here: 'ye shall dwell in the land that I gave to your fathers.' 'I want you to be where I first put you. That's where you've got to come back to.' And now watch the marvel and the wonder of the way in which he does it.

First of all, we need to be cleansed. That is why you must always start with the cross, with the blood of Christ. It is no good talking about communion with God unless you go via the cross. It is no use talking about living a holy life or about understanding spiritual truth unless you start there. What God does first of all is to cleanse us, to wash us, to get rid of this filth that is obviously upon us. That is always the beginning.

There is no point in our proceeding unless we are clear about that. There is no way to God except via Calvary. There is no knowledge of God except in Jesus Christ and him crucified. That is why Christ came, and why he had to die. That is why, when Peter said to him, 'Be it far from thee, Lord: this shall not be unto thee', he turned to him and said, 'Get thee behind me, Satan ... thou savourest not the things that be of God, but those that be of men' (Matt. 16:22, 23). The disciples did not like this idea of the cross. They did their utmost to stop him going there. They pleaded with him not to go. They said, 'If you go to Jerusalem, they'll kill you.' But he set his face to go to Jerusalem and to die. He came to die. He said, 'The Son of man came not to be ministered unto, but to minister, and to give his life a ransom for many' (Matt. 20:28).

You have got to start there. And then you need this new mind and understanding: there is another step. And then, after that, you have got to become holy, so he proceeds to make us holy. Then, God having done all that to us, comes the final thing: we are ushered into his presence. You see it is the exact reversal of what happened in the fall.

The apostle John puts it like this: 'For this purpose the Son of God was manifested, that he might destroy'—bring to naught, cancel out—'the works of the devil' (1 John 3:8). And those are the works of the devil, in that order. So the Son of God came and died, and he cancelled them out one by one, and the final one is this: 'You shall be to me a people and I will be to you a God; I will be your God.'

I wonder whether we realize that this is the highest thing of all, the ultimate of salvation.

If I asked you to give me a definition of Christian salvation—What is it? What does it mean?—I wonder whether you would have gone on to this, the highest point, the acme, the very zenith.

Do you know why the Lord Jesus Christ died? The apostle Peter says that it was 'that he might bring us to God' (1 Pet. 3:18). That is the object of it all. It stops at nothing short of that. And yet how often do we all stop short of this! Had you realized that this is the ultimate thing: that we are brought into such a relationship with God that he says to us, 'You are my people,' and that we can turn to God and say, '*My* God, *my* God'?

Oh, how we insult God by leaving this out! We are interested in particular gifts and particular blessings. We say, 'Yes, I am interested in this Christianity because a certain sin gets me down and I can't get rid of it. Now, if Christianity can help me to get over that sin, I want it.' So we go in for Christianity to get over that sin. We say, 'Ah, it's gone. Thank God!' We give our testimony about how we got rid of the sin, and we stop at that.

Or we may be afraid of death. We may be afraid of the judgment. We may be deeply aware of our sins and we know we have got to stand before God. And we say, 'What I want is forgiveness of sins. I hear the message about Christ. I say I'll accept it. Christ died for me. My sins are forgiven. Thank God! All is well. I can go on happily.'

Others need other particular blessings: healing of their body, perhaps, friendship, a sense of sympathy, and so on. All these things are in the gospel, thank God. But if we stop at any one of them, we are insulting God. We have left out the most important thing of all. We are interested in the gifts and we have not said a word about the Giver himself.

We would all like to get back into Paradise, into the garden of Eden, so that we do not have to work and we have plenty of food and sunshine and all that is easy and happy. And we have said not a word about the One who comes down into the garden to visit us and to talk to us directly and immediately. Yet that is the most wonderful, the most glorious thing of all: that we are brought back into the fellowship that was broken, into the knowledge of God that man lost by his fall and by the folly of his sin.

That is the very thing which Ezekiel tells us at this point. He has been leading us up to it. That is why I must be cleansed from my filthiness: no filthiness can stand there. That is why I must have spiritual understanding: carnal ideas are of no value in the presence of God. That is why I must be holy: 'I am holy; be ye holy', says the Lord. How can I stand before that burning light if there is iniquity within me?

But all these steps have simply been preparatory. Imagine somebody who, having received an invitation to an audience with the Queen in Buckingham Palace, buys the uniform or the dress, and consults the books of etiquette. That person gets all the instruction, makes all the preparations, and then does not turn up at Buckingham Palace, but is content simply with having bought the dress or the suit and admiring himself or herself in the garb, but never availing him- or herself of the privilege of having the audience. That is precisely what we all tend to do with God. We forget that the ultimate purpose of this great salvation is to bring us to this knowledge of God that we have lost because of our sin.

How does this happen? Let us follow the steps as they are outlined here. Someone might say, 'But surely there's something wrong with all this. It says "Ye shall be my people and I will be your God." Isn't God the God of the whole world? Are not all the people that are on the earth the people of God? Are not all under his hand? Isn't he the Lord God Almighty, the God of all the universe, the whole cosmos?' The answer, of course, is that he is. God reigns. He is over all. He sits upon the throne of the universe and all things are under his hands. So are not all people therefore his people?

The answer to that is very simple, and the Old Testament brings it out very clearly. All the nations of the world were under God, under his power and his sovereignty. And yet he says through the prophet Amos to the children of Israel, 'You only have I known of all the families [or nations] of the earth' (Amos 3:2). He knew about all others, but he knew these in a special manner. That is what we have here. Yes, God is the judge, the God of the whole world and the entire universe. And there are men and women in the world today who say they do not believe in God and are not interested in him but who nevertheless will have to stand in the holy presence of God and find that he is God. But that is not what Ezekiel is talking about.

Clearly, there is something limiting in this, something which is restricted, special. What is it? It is the supreme blessing of all. Let us look at it as it is put to us. The first thing we are told is 'Ye shall be my people.' Here is God speaking. Let us look at it for a moment from God's side.

Do you realize what is offered to you today in the gospel of the Lord Jesus Christ? You are offered the opportunity to become one of God's people. What an offer! What does it mean? Let us go back and work it out in terms of this Old Testament history. It is all shown there very perfectly. There were all the nations of the world; they were all God's nations.

He was the God of them all. But God began to do something wonderful. He took hold of a man called Abram and said to him, 'I am going to change your name and call you Abraham. I am going to make of you a nation. Out of you and out of your loins shall come a nation greater in number than the sand of the seashore. I am going to make a nation for myself. These nations have turned against me. They have turned their backs, they have forsaken me and my holy laws. I am going to make a nation for myself, my own people, and I am going to do it in you and out of you.' And he did it: he created a nation for himself, his people. He put them in a special position, apart from everybody else.

And so, when he brought them out of the captivity of Egypt, he gave them the Ten Commandments. He told them, 'You are a holy nation, a peculiar people, a people for my own special possession. I own everything. All the nations are mine, but not like you. You are my own private possession.'

The apostle Peter applies these very words to all who are Christians:

> Ye are a chosen generation, a royal priesthood, an holy nation, a peculiar people; that ye should shew forth the praises of him who hath called you out of darkness into his marvellous light; which in time past were not a people, but are now the people of God: which had not obtained mercy, but now have obtained mercy. Dearly beloved, I beseech you as strangers and pilgrims, abstain from fleshly lusts, which war against the soul; having your conversation honest among the Gentiles: that, whereas they speak against you as evildoers, they may by your good works, which they shall behold, glorify God in the day of visitation (1 Pet. 2:9-12).

Notice '[you] were not a people, but are now the people of God; which had not obtained mercy, but now have obtained mercy'. What are you? 'A chosen generation, a royal priesthood, an holy nation, a peculiar people'—which means a people for God's own private, personal possession. This is the very thing that is said to us in the gospel of Jesus Christ today.

The terrible final truth about all who are not Christians is that they are not a people. They are just an indiscriminate rabble. They are outside the promises of God. They are strangers to his covenant. If men and women could only realize this, they would not stay there for a second. There is nothing more terrible than to be without God in the world, outsiders, bearing no relationship to God, just living as human beings—indeed, at times as animals—belonging to a realm that is dying and decaying, and that will go to perdition and everlasting suffering. That is the position. They are lost in a movement, in a mass. And the tragedy is that they delight in that. They hate the idea of being under the eye of God. They want to get away from God, to lose themselves in the crowd.

What a terrible thing that is. I can imagine nothing more terrible today than to be in that condition in which I am altogether outside the life of the eternal God, as if he did not exist; lost, without God, without hope in the world.

But the most wonderful thing about being a Christian is the converse: that in Christ we become the people of God, his peculiar possession, his special treasure. Just as God made the nation of Israel and set them on one side for himself, so he does with all who are Christians. We become members of this new holy nation, this royal priesthood. We are what Israel was: the new people of God. And that means that we are separated from the mass which is not a people. God puts us into a position entirely apart, not because we are better, not because we have done anything wonderful or better than other people, but simply because we have seen where we were and we have been alarmed, have believed God and accepted the message, and therefore he delivers us. It is not because of the lives we are living; no, it is because we have seen that we are vile sinners and that we are going to hell. The others think they are marvellous. They are the Pharisees. But we, as the publican, have come to see ourselves in our sins and in our rags. God makes us his own people, and this is the most comforting thing I know today: that I belong to the people of God, and that I am not in the world and I am not going to be lost with it and go to perdition with it. God has separated me and put me into this new position.

Our verse says 'ye shall be *my* people', and that means that we have become the objects of his special attention, his special interest, his special concern. If you know of anything better or greater than that, I would like to know what it is! It is staggering, almost incredible! But it is everywhere in the Bible. The Lord Jesus Christ says that the very hairs of our head are all numbered: that is the sort of interest that God takes in those who believe in the Lord Jesus Christ and belong to him. Nothing, he says, can happen to you without your Father. If this great God knows when every sparrow falls to the ground, how much greater is his interest in you, you whom he has bought and separated unto himself even at the cost of the shed blood of his only begotten Son. This is what makes salvation so glorious! Yes, I thank God for every particular blessing; but the thing that comforts me today is to know that the everlasting and eternal God knows me, is looking on me and is interested in me as an individual person.

I do not want to be lost in the mob. What I like to be told is, 'I will guide thee with mine eye' (Psa. 32:8); to be told that this infinite, glorious Person is interested in me and that nothing can happen to me apart from him. That is the way to meet life and to master it. That is the way to conquer your phobias, your fears and all your alarms: to know that you are in God's hands and that he takes this eternal loving interest in you. And that is what is offered in the gospel. That is Christianity: God looking on you in particular and making a special object of interest of you.

But then it goes on: because of all this, I know that God has a purpose with respect to me. He has a purpose with respect to everyone who is a Christian.

I have already said that this is a supernatural, miraculous work and God never does anything by halves. He does not start a work and give it up. When God starts a work, he always finishes it, and therefore I know today that in Christ not only am I forgiven, not only have all my sins and trans-gressions been blotted out, not only am I justified, not only is he sanctifying me, not only is he working in me in order to deliver me from the power of sin as well as its guilt—but I know that he will go on with it and that nothing can stop it. I am able to say with the apostle Paul that 'neither death, nor life, nor angels, nor principalities, nor powers, nor things present, nor things to come, nor height, nor depth, nor any other creature, shall be able to separate us from the love of God, which is in Christ Jesus our Lord' (Rom. 8:38, 39).

There is nothing comparable to this: to know that God has got his eye on you, that he has put his hand on you, that he has taken you out of that mass of perdition and is fashioning you and forming you for himself, and that he is going to bring you to glory. 'Whom he called, them he also justified: and whom he justified, them he also glorified' (Rom. 8:30). Paul sees the end from the beginning, and in God's hand, as one of his people, I know that I am being taken there. Let the world do its worst, let hell rage, let men kill my body: it can never separate me from the love of God which is in Christ Jesus our Lord. 'Ye shall be *my* people.'

But look at it from our side for a moment. 'Ye shall be my people, and I will be your God.' What does this mean? It does not mean that you can just have a general belief in God. You can have a general belief in God and not be a Christian. It does not mean that you can have a bit of a general knowledge about God; again, you can have that without being a Christian. According to the apostle Paul, we all ought to have that by deducing from what we see in nature and in creation, in history and in providence. Knowledge of the existence of an eternal creator, of a great mind behind the universe: that is not the knowledge that Ezekiel is speaking about here. There are many who have got that. No, what he means is that we have a personal knowledge, an immediate, direct knowledge: that we no longer only know about God, but that we really get to know God. Adam knew God. He spoke to God. God came down into the garden and spoke to the man and the woman, and they spoke to him. They knew him. But because of sin, that knowledge was lost. We all retain a knowledge about God. But in salvation, you do not stop at that. The Lord Jesus Christ himself uttered these words: 'This is life eternal, that they might know thee the only true God, and Jesus Christ whom thou hast sent' (John 17:3).

My God. It is not merely that I say, 'I believe there is a God, a great God in the heavens who is the ruler of the ends of the earth, the judge eternal. I believe in his creatorship, his power.' No, he is *my* God, my personal God, the God whom I know and to whom I speak as person to person. That is what the gospel of Jesus Christ gives. And what does that lead to?

First, it gives you an assurance of his personal interest in you. Have you got that? Do you know it? Do you know that

God is interested in you? Are you aware of it? Can you say, 'O Love that wilt not let me go'? Have you had that feeling? In your folly you would have gone from him, you would have turned to sin and to other things. But he would not let you go. He came after you because you belong to him, because you are one of his people and he is your God. Do you know that? Have you got that assurance that God is your God; that you belong to him?

Then, of course, it gives you a wonderful confidence when you go to him in prayer. This is the test, is it not? We all know what it is. We get into trouble, or something goes wrong, an illness, an accident or some awful problem. Everything has been tried and has failed. And we say, 'Oh, let's try prayer.' And you go on your knees and you cannot speak—for this reason: you feel you do not know God. You are full of doubts, hesitations and uncertainties. You seem to cry out in the dark. But what is offered here in the gospel does away with that. You go into his presence and you say, '*My* God, I come to thee.' The psalmist puts it perfectly in Psalm 42: 'My soul thirsteth for God, for the living God … who is the health of my countenance.' My God, in whom I will trust.

Read the lives of all the saints who have ever lived and you will find that that is the thing they rejoiced in, above everything else. 'When my father and my mother forsake me, then the LORD will take me up' (Psa. 27:10). Is there anything more wonderful in this world than that? 'When all things seem against us, to drive us to despair, I know one gate is open, one ear will hear my prayer.' Is that your position?

And then, of course, it leads to this final assurance that, whatever my position, whatever my predicament, all the power of God is behind me. He is eternal. He is everlasting. He is invincible. His resources are illimitable. And if he is my

God, all that is behind me. And he has promised, 'I will never leave thee, nor forsake thee' (Heb. 13:5). Is not this the one thing that this uncertain world needs above everything today? Old age coming on, illness, accident, disappointment, friends betraying you, everything going wrong, the third world war, hell let loose, everything collapsing, but still the ability to say, '*My* God, thou art still with me and thou wilt never leave me. I know that I am in thy hands and that nothing can ever separate me from thee. Nothing can ever take me out of thy grasp and out of thine eternal grip.' Oh, the safety of that position: of the knowledge that, whatever this world, this life, may do to us, our eternal future is guaranteed in the hands of God! In Christ we are brought into 'an inheritance incorruptible, and undefiled, and that fadeth not away, reserved in heaven' for us by God (1 Pet. 1:4). 'You are my people', and God is *our* God.

Can you say, '*My* God?' Do you know him personally? That is what Christ came to give you: not only forgiveness, not only new understanding, not only cleansing and holiness, but all that in order that we might be enabled to go into the holiest of all with full assurance of faith and know that we will always be there. Have you got that? Are you in that position? That is Christianity. That is the ultimate of it; the acme, the glory of it. He gave himself for us that he might bring us to God.

10. Man in a State of Famine

I will also save you from all your uncleannesses: and I will call for the corn, and will increase it, and lay no famine upon you. And I will multiply the fruit of the tree, and the increase of the field, that ye shall receive no more reproach of famine among the heathen.—Ezekiel 36:29, 30

WE have seen that all the steps and stages of salvation lead up to this: to bring us to God. That is the supreme blessing: 'Ye shall be my people, and I will be your God.' There is nothing beyond that. The supreme blessing is to come into that relationship with God in which you can say, 'My God; my God, thou art mine and I am thine.'

All that God has done in Jesus Christ and all the application of it by the Holy Spirit is designed to bring us to just that, to fit us and prepare us for it. But the prophet does not stop there; the word 'also' at the beginning of verse 29 reminds us that we are continuing the theme. Having brought us to that topmost point, he goes on. What is he going to show us now? He is going to show us some of the things that result from that.

You see how simple this gospel is. Our real need is just to know God. And if we know God, all our other subsidiary needs will be dealt with and satisfied. This is always the order. The children of Israel had been in a state of famine. They did not like famine; they wanted plenty, and their great cry was for plenty. But you cannot have plenty except from God, so the great need was to know how to come to God. And it is exactly the same today. The world is in trouble. There are certain particular needs, but its tragedy is that it does not know the cause of all this, which is our need of God. So if we are interested in particular blessings, we need to discover how to arrive at God and to know that he is our God and we are his people. The way is through Jesus Christ and him crucified: the Christ who has borne our punishment, has died in our stead and has reconciled us to God, and who then gives us new life and the power of the Holy Spirit, and brings us into the presence of God, washed, cleansed, reconciled and renewed.

Having reached that point, we can begin to consider the particular blessings. They are put for us here in these two verses. Notice that this prophet puts them in terms of material blessings. He talks about calling for the corn and increasing it so that there may be no famine. God will also multiply the fruit of the trees and the increase of the field. Here is an important and very interesting principle: blessings from God in the Old Testament are generally put in that material form and manner. God, if I may so put it with reverence, spoke to the people in a manner they could understand. So God's blessings in the Old Testament are generally in terms of a great crop of corn, fruit trees full of fruit, a great abundance of sheep, cattle, oxen and camels, and so on. That is how people estimated their blessing at the hand of God. It was God's way of accommodating himself to the ignorance and the frailty of the people.

But in addition to being true in the Old Testament dispensation, it was also a foreshadowing of a very much higher type of blessing that was going to come: the spiritual blessings of salvation that come in and through our Lord and Saviour, Jesus Christ. So as you read your Old Testament and hear about all the corn, the fruit, the fruit of the vine, and so on, remember that it is a pictorial way of representing these mighty, glorious, spiritual blessings that God offers to all who believe in his only Son, our Lord and Saviour Jesus Christ.

So what is the result of salvation? What is it that I can look forward to, having come to God in and through the Lord Jesus Christ? Let me summarize it by putting it like this: I come to a place of fullness of blessing. I come to a place of all-sufficiency. I come to a place of final satisfaction. The salvation which is obtainable in the Lord Jesus Christ is a full and gloriously abundant salvation. And there is literally no end to the blessings that it has to offer to us.

I suggest that there is no aspect of the Christian life that is so missed or so frequently misunderstood as that. Ask the average person today why he is not a Christian and he will probably say something like this: 'Christianity, you say? Most certainly not!' 'Why?' you ask. 'Well,' he says, 'it's so narrow. It's such a small life. It's such a cramped, miserable, uninteresting life.' The average person's idea of Christianity is that it calls you to give up things and gives you nothing in return. To use words from Milton's *Lycidas*, it is a life which calls you to 'scorn delights, and live laborious days': miserable, narrow, cramped, confined, taking away on all hands and giving nothing in return. They say, 'No self-respecting man intellectually can possibly be a Christian.' They say, 'Christianity confines you to one book and you shut out everything else. It has nothing to give you intellectually. You just become a fool, an ignoramus. This sort of thing flourishes amongst ignorant illiterate people, but there's nothing to give to the sophisticated, to the cultured. Intellectually, it's nowhere. It's got nothing. It just makes you say goodbye to your intellect.'

And they say exactly the same thing about it in the realm of feelings and emotions. The world is interested, they say, in love, in the exercise of emotions. And they feel that Christianity is so miserable, so sad, so drab, so dull, so uninteresting. And then they say, 'For the imagination, what's it got to give? When you go to the world, why, your imagination is always being stimulated! You get it in poetry, films, plays, novels; always new horizons opened out. The realm of the imagination—there's no end to it! How wonderful it is! Nothing like that in Christianity; the same old thing: held down, kept in, cramped, confined.' They have a feeling that this Christian life is an entirely negative sort of life and that there is nothing large and full about it; there is nothing positive.

Most people reject Christianity for themselves for that reason. There are some who have become very concerned about certain persons who are very dear to them and whom they love very much and who have become Christians. They feel 'they are just shutting themselves out from life'; 'they're going to live a small, little life. They are going to miss so much.' They are concerned that they are entering into this narrow little world. Indeed, most people today seem to reject Christianity in terms of what they call 'life'. It is because they want life, they say, and a full life, a great life, that they have no use for this Christian life.

But our text says the exact opposite. It seems to suggest that it is the other life that is the life of famine, of need, of want, and that Christianity is the life of riches, of blessing and of superabundance. Therefore I put as my first principle just this: the sinful life, the godless life, the life that is independent of God and does not look to him, is a life that always and invariably leads to famine. Here it is in our text: 'I will also save you from all your uncleannesses: and I will call for the corn, and will increase it, and will lay no famine upon you.' And he goes on to say: 'And I will multiply the fruit of the tree, and the increase of the field.' Why? 'That ye shall receive no more reproach of famine among the heathen.' This is what had happened: the children of Israel, because of their disobedience of God, had been in a state of famine. And all the heathen nations had looked at them and said, 'Ah, there are a people who said they were God's people. Look at them: they're starving. They are in a state of famine.' But God says, 'No longer shall you be in a state of famine when I have done all this to you. I will shower my blessings upon you.'

Our Lord stated it perfectly for us in the parable of the prodigal son, who left home with his pockets full of money but found himself in a land which was visited by famine. 'There arose a mighty famine in that land' (Luke 15:14), the far-off land to which he had gone, which he had said was so much better than his homeland, the land for which he had forsaken father and brother and home and everything else. He began to be in want, and eventually he reached the point of starvation.

How often it happened to the children of Israel! It was their disobedience of God, their violating of his laws, that always rendered them into this condition of famine. And is there anything more obvious in our world today than the appalling famine of the days in which we live—not in terms of food or material things, but in the realm of the spiritual? People talk about the atomic bomb and the hydrogen bomb, but there is something much more appalling than all that: it is the spiritual famine in which men and women are living, the appalling famine and starvation of life apart from God.

Let me show you what I mean. For those who are not in communion with God, this famine is quite inevitable, because the very type of life they live leads to famine. If the Bible is right—and it is—when it says that man and woman were made by God and for God, obviously man and woman without God must be in need. They must be in a state in which they are deprived of that which is most valuable. They are in a state of famine or starvation, by definition. How poor they are! How deprived! How starved! And it is the whole case of the Bible to say that anyone who is not in communion with God and being blessed by God is in a state of spiritual starvation, of necessity.

But there is a second thing which makes this inevitable: God finally withholds his blessings from those who do not seek him. That is exactly what he did with the children of Israel. They said they could get on without God. They began worshipping other gods. 'Very well,' said God, 'carry on'; and he withheld his blessings. And there they were, starving, in a state of famine.

The most appalling thing that can ever happen to a human being is to be abandoned by God. There is an awful word in the book of the prophet Hosea where God says this about Ephraim: 'Ephraim rejoices in his sin. Let him alone. Leave him to himself', abandoned of God. As the apostle Paul puts it in the first chapter of his epistle to the Romans, when mankind in its folly and its ignorance in sin got to a certain point, 'God gave them up', 'God gave them over to a reprobate mind' (Rom. 1:24, 26, 28). He just withdrew his blessings and his control. That is what is happening in the modern world: God is leaving men and women to themselves. They have said they do not want him. 'Very well,' says God, 'get on without me.' That is why famine is inevitable.

Let me try to show you some of the characteristics of this famine. Let us look at it in practice, in operation. Life without God is a starved life, a life of famine, first of all with respect to the mind and the intellect. 'Surely,' says someone, 'you are not going to say that this present generation is a generation that is starved in the realm of mind and intellect?' Well, as I read the newspapers and the reports that they give of what is being said by librarians when they meet in conference, I am beginning to think this is true. The librarians tell us that people are no longer anxious to read. They do not go for books as they used to. They are not even reading novels. They say they cannot read; the mind does not seem to be capable of it.

There was a time when people could listen to speeches, addresses, lectures and sermons which might go on for an hour or longer. We are told today that the modern man and woman cannot stand it. They cannot take it in. We are told that they cannot concentrate for more than twenty minutes. So we are supposed to break it up and have pauses and a little music to give relief. The minds of people today cannot stand the strain. Those are the facts.

It seems to me that the minds of men and women are being starved. What is the matter? Why are their minds like this? Why can they not take in truth? Why has everything got to be spoon-fed today? Why has it got to be so simple and so elementary? Why cannot people follow argument and reason and logic? In the past they could, and they revelled in it. Read the speeches of the statesmen. Read the sermons of the preachers. The people rejoiced in all this. But people today say, 'It isn't so much that I don't like it; I can't do it.' Does it not look as if the human intellect is being starved?

When people turn away from God their minds always begin to degenerate. I could prove it to you historically time without number. Did you know that when this country has been most religious it has been most intellectual? That is a simple fact. Our popular modern education is a direct outcome of the Evangelical Revival of the eighteenth century. Something similar happened after the Protestant Reformation and again in the Puritan revival of the seventeenth century. When people turn to God, their minds begin to open out. When they go away from God, they stop using their minds; and that is what is happening today. They say they cannot read or listen to sermons. They can only look at pictures. They can only look at the television. They can only work out football pools. Is that intellectual? The godless life starves the mind. Whatever else goes when people turn from God, true intellectual life and activity disappears.

In exactly the same way, turning away from God starves the moral nature. There are people in the world today who do not know what morality means. I do not condemn them; I am sorry for them. It is because they are godless, because they are out of touch with God. They see no wrong in what they are doing. They misuse their bodies; they abuse them. They are guilty of foul perversions. They see no wrong in them. And they are quite honest and sincere. But what is the matter with them? They are what we call today 'amoral'. Those who are immoral know that they are wrong; they have a sense of morals. The trouble today is that people do not even have a sense of morals; it means nothing to them. They almost do not have a moral nature; it is starved.

You see this when you read the newspapers. And it is evident not only in the matters of the flesh, physical matters, but also in moral judgment in the political world and internationally: convenience, anything that happens to suit. We will drop our principles, we will change our coats, we will do anything in order to have an easy and a good time. Compromise is the rule of the day and the old standards have gone. Things have been tolerated in this twentieth century that no one would have dreamt of tolerating a hundred years ago. What a decline in the realm of morals is to be seen in politics and in every other realm of life.

And, finally, the heart is starved. This is one of the real tragedies of this present age which talks so much about the heart and is so interested in the emotions and love. As I read the newspapers and see what is happening, I say to myself, 'The real trouble with these people is they don't know what love is.' They do not. They are just fascinated for the moment with some infatuation. If they only knew what it was to be in love, they would not behave like this. They would not be passing like this in series through the divorce courts and so on. Again, I do not condemn them; I am sorry for them. They are starved emotionally. They do not know what love is. Their emotional nature has been so deprived, neglected, starved, that they do not begin to understand these things.

All along the line and in every department the godless life leads to starvation. When things go wrong you see more clearly the state of starvation that people are in: there is nothing to turn to, no one to go to, no consolation to fall back upon, nothing to assuage the grief, nothing to give some compensation. So they fly to drink or drugs. They have to; they cannot stand it; they would break down otherwise. Is there anything that so proves the utter appalling starvation of people in a spiritual sense as the way in which they are entirely dependent upon artificial stimulants of various kinds? And when they come finally to look at death and the end, they are without hope; they have nothing at all to speak to them, their minds, their hearts, their moral nature; there is nothing behind them, nothing in the moment, nothing to look forward to; it is a blank. The godless life leads to starvation.

There is a beautiful word in the New Testament that sums it all up. We are told that our blessed Lord and Saviour Jesus Christ looked at the people who were around him and that he was grieved in heart because he saw them 'as sheep having no shepherd' (Matt. 9:36). He did not condemn them; he felt a heart of compassion for them. He came from heaven because of them. 'As sheep without a shepherd': there is a great abundance of grass, but the sheep do not know it, and they do not have a shepherd to lead them to it. They are dashing about trying to find a blade here and there. They are living in a wilderness. Oh, how horrible! How sad!

That is the modern world. And that is why the heart of every Christian should be full of compassion for men and women who think that they are living a marvellous life but who are revealing the fact that they are in a state of starvation, with their over-stimulated eyes, their nerves on end, the breakdowns and all the other things that follow. It is the sinful life that leads to famine and starvation. It is the Christian life that leads to blessing, satisfaction and super-abundance. 'I will call for the corn, and will increase it ... I will multiply the fruit of the tree, and the increase of the field.' And, blessed be the name of God, he does.

The men of the Old Testament knew something about this. Listen to Psalm 23: 'The LORD is my shepherd; I shall not want.' What a contrast! 'He maketh me to lie down in green pastures; he leadeth me beside the still waters. He restoreth my soul ... Thou preparest a table before me in the presence of mine enemies.'

David knew what he was talking about. He had had a shot of both types of life, and that is what he said. He said it again

in Psalm 84. 'As a man,' he says, 'who has got a bit of experience in this world, I tell you I had rather be a doorkeeper in
the house of my God, than to dwell in the tents of wickedness.'
He would prefer to stand and be the doorkeeper, giving out
hymnbooks in the vestibule, than be at the very centre of the
life of the ungodly. Why? Because he knows that the life of the
ungodly, though it appears to be wonderful at first, is just the
life that robs you. It takes from you. It exhausts you and leaves
you as a wreck in the end. That is what you get in the tents of
the ungodly: exhaustion, emaciation and final hopelessness.

But the threshold of God's house, the very vestibule, is a
rather wonderful place; he says, 'I can peep in through the
door sometimes and have a glimpse at the glory. The Lord
God is a sun and a shield.' Grace and glory, just a glimpse of
it—how marvellous! 'A day in thy courts,' he says, 'is better
than a thousand.' What satisfaction this life gives!

If you want to see it all again in detail, read Hebrews 11,
where you will be given a sort of analysis of the life of those
Old Testament saints and heroes. You could sum it all up in
the words that we are told about Moses: '... choosing rather
to suffer affliction with the people of God, than to enjoy the
pleasures of sin for a season' (verse 25). He had his eye on the
reward.

The New Testament is full of it. Our Lord himself says to
the woman of Samaria, 'Whosoever drinketh of this water'—
the water in the physical well—'shall thirst again: but whosoever drinketh of the water that I shall give him shall never
thirst; but the water that I shall give him shall be in him a well
of water springing up into everlasting life' (John 4:13, 14).
What an abundance!

Listen to him saying it again in John 6:35: 'He that cometh
to me shall *never* hunger; and he that believeth on me shall

never thirst.' Narrow, cramped, depriving? Not at all! He says it again in John 10 when talking about his sheep: they 'shall go in and out, and find pasture ... I am come that they might have life, and that they might have it more abundantly' (verses 9, 10).

Is it true in practice? If it were not true, I would not be standing in this pulpit at this moment. I rejoice to say that if I have no other reason for being a Christian than the sheer intellectual satisfaction that it gives me, it will be enough for me. I know of nothing that is comparable to the Bible. There is intellectual satisfaction as I look at God's plan of making the world and his purpose with respect to it, and as I see the fall coming in, apparently wrecking it, and then God initiating the movement of salvation. In some way I am a student of history and of philosophy. I am interested in mankind, the working of the human mind and brain, this world and what is happening in it, and politics. And it is because of that that I am a Christian, because it is only here that I find a satisfactory answer to my questions and a philosophy that really holds water. It is only here that I begin to understand history and what is happening. I have tried the others; I still read them. But they have given me nothing. They raise questions—they are brilliant at putting questions—but I am more interested in answers than in questions. And for my answers, I always have to come to this book.

If you are not a Christian, believe me, your mind has not started working yet. That is your real trouble: the content is too small; the pabulum is not sufficient; the scope, the plan, is not big enough. You are living in a little section. We are all experts sitting on some little branch of knowledge. Come, I say, and have the whole philosophy of God. You have got it in this book; begin to study it and apply your mind to it. You will be amazed at the results that will follow. Your mind will begin to develop and expand. You will take in and encompass various realms. You will be amazed at yourself and at the intellectual satisfaction.

One of my great problems in life is to find sufficient time to read this book, and to read the works of men who have written about it. If I had no conscience and were not a bit concerned about other men and women whom I know are dying in sin and whom I see as sheep without a shepherd, I would shut myself up in libraries and spend the rest of my days just reading: reading the Puritans, reading about Wesley and Whitefield and the men of the eighteenth century, and grappling with these tremendous commentaries on this final truth. And even then I would die feeling that I had not even started.

Oh, if you are not Christian, you have no idea how you are starving your mind, your brain and your intellect! And obviously it does the same for one's moral nature. Here it is in verse 29: 'I will also save you from all your uncleannesses.' You see, though you are a Christian, though you believe Christ has died for you, though you are born again and though the Holy Spirit is in you, you will still find uncleannesses in you. And you will be worried, troubled and unhappy about it. And you will say, 'Oh, how can I get rid of these?' You will only find the answer in this same marvellous gospel of salvation. It is by the power of the Holy Spirit that you will be delivered from your particular sins. As you look into the face of Christ and read his life, you see what man should be, how one should walk through this vile world. And you want to be like him, and so you go on and follow him. As you do so, your moral nature begins to develop and expand, and you grow in grace and in the knowledge of the Lord.

And, of course, it does the same for your emotional nature. If men and women only knew something about this! If you only knew something about the joy of salvation! I understand the psalmist very well: 'A day in thy courts is better than a thousand ...' I would almost give up a lifetime for certain blessed experiences that God in his mercy has vouchsafed me. Do you know what it is to be moved to the very depths of your being? Wordsworth, in a mystical sense, was able to say: 'To me the meanest flower that blows can give thoughts that do often lie too deep for tears.' But if he had only known something of this, he would have known something altogether deeper, bigger and mightier than that: the joy, the peace, the satisfaction, the emotional content. Read your hymns. Look at those men: were they simply indulging in fancy? No, they had experienced it; they were enjoying these things. That is why they wrote their experiences in their hymns. 'Thou, O Christ, art all I want,' says Charles Wesley. 'More than all in thee I find ... Plenteous grace with thee is found.' 'O for a thousand tongues to sing my great Redeemer's praise!' There is love, joy, peace and all these other glorious emotions.

But you see it most of all—and this is the final proof—when you are face to face with circumstances. Our Lord was a realist. He knew what it was to suffer. But he said, 'He that cometh to me shall never hunger; and he that believeth on me shall never thirst' (John 6:35). Do you know that is the literal truth? It does not matter what is happening; if you go to Christ, you will no longer hunger or thirst. Whatever your need is, whatever your lack, whatever your lack of satisfaction, go to Christ; and I assure you that you will no longer be hungry and you will no longer thirst. He will more than satisfy you.

Are you facing trials, tribulations and adversities? Are you
hemmed in by problems and difficulties? This is what the
apostle Paul, speaking directly out of a life of great hardships
and sufferings, says to you in Philippians 4:6, 7: 'In nothing
be anxious'—in nothing allow yourself to be killed by anxious
care and to be crushed by anxiety—'but in all things'—it does
not matter what—'with prayer and supplication and thanksgiving let your requests be made known unto God. And the
peace of God that passeth all understanding shall keep your
heart and mind in Christ Jesus.' You will be amazed at yourself. You will be astonished when you wake up in the morning
that you could possibly have slept with such terrible problems confronting you. But you will. 'The peace of God that
passeth all understanding will keep your hearts and minds.'
(Phil. 4:7) It will act as a garrison around them so that as the
anxious thoughts come, they will be shut out. And your heart
and your mind will enjoy that blessed peace and rest. Listen
to him as he goes on: 'I have learned, in whatsoever state I
am, therewith to be content. I know both how to be abased,
and I know how to abound' (4:11, 12). He is independent
of circumstances. 'I can do all things through Christ which
strengtheneth me' (verse 13). He never fails.

What about death? Death is the last enemy, the final problem—but not to the Christian. 'To me,' says Paul, 'to live is
Christ, and to die is gain, for it means going to be with Christ,
which is far better.' 'My hope I cannot measure; my path to
life is free. My Saviour has my treasure, and he will walk with
me.'

Oh, the abounding character of this blessed life in Christ!
Oh, the glory of it all! Yes, the corn is abounding, the fruit
tree is laden with fruit, the earth is giving her increase. My
every need is satisfied: my intellect, my heart, my moral

nature. Whatever circumstances or chance may bring, it is all right; I am given a new way of looking at them. I am given a new understanding. I am given a philosophy that can see through it. Death, the end, everything: I see through it all. And I look to eternity, where there is reserved for all who are in Christ an inheritance incorruptible and undefiled, and that fadeth not away, reserved by God in heaven for all who are in Christ.

Are you enjoying this richness, this blessing? Are you aware of this satisfaction in Christ? Do you know the peace of God that passes all understanding when everything has gone against you? Can you say that you never hunger and never thirst? What of your intellectual life? What of your moral life? What of your emotional life? Are you being satisfied? How are you standing up to life?

If you are failing in this, there is only one explanation: you do not know God. For if you know God, if God is your God and you are God's child, you will know the satisfaction. So if you have not got the satisfaction, it is simply because you do not know God. And why do you not know God? It may be that you have never realized you are a sinner. It may be that you have never seen any meaning or sense in the bread and the wine, that you see no purpose in the death of Christ upon the cross and the shedding of his blood. You need to go right back to the first step; for once you know God, you will know satisfaction.

Start by simply going to God and confessing your sin. Ask him by his Spirit to make you realize your sin as you have never done before. Ask him to give you the new nature and the new life. Ask him to give you his Spirit in his fullness. If you do so genuinely, he will answer. And you will begin to know this blessed life of God.

If you have felt that, like the prodigal, you are in some strange, far-off land where there is nothing but famine, and that you are bereft and starving in the vitals of your being, hasten today to Jesus Christ, who is waiting and willing and ready to receive you. And he will lead you to God and introduce you to the abundance, the life which is life indeed, that he has to give. Hasten to him.

11. The Foolishness of Man

Then shall ye remember your own evil ways, and your doings that were not good, and shall lothe yourselves in your own sight for your iniquities and for your abominations. Not for your sakes do I this, saith the Lord GOD, be it known unto you: be ashamed and confounded for your own ways, O house of Israel. —Ezekiel 36:31, 32

IT is important that we should know what the gospel is in its various steps and stages, not only so that we may come to enjoy its incomparable blessings, but also so that we may be taught how to distinguish between that which is true and that which is false.

Mankind, as a result of sin, is in a state of misery. We are all unhappy. There is no such thing, as the poets have often reminded us, as perfect happiness in a world like this. Dryden tells us, 'Every man who lives is born to die, and none can boast sincere felicity.' In this world there is always a fly in the ointment: always something wrong, something that detracts and tends to spoil everything. The world and its peoples are in trouble, and we are seeking for solutions, looking for happiness, peace and joy. Nobody likes to be miserable.

And the great message of the Bible is that God has done something about that. He has provided his gospel, the way of deliverance and emancipation. He has even sent his only Son from heaven to earth, and to the death of the cross, in order to do that.

But, alas, there is somebody else who is also trying to do something about it.

The devil, the great antagonist of God, in his hatred of God and his desire to spoil God's universe and to wreck the perfection which it once had, comes along and offers his proposals with regard to the solution of our various problems. Nothing, therefore, is quite so important for us as to learn how to differentiate between the true and the false: between that which is God's way and these other spurious ways, these other gospels which, as Paul says, are no gospels, but which come in such a pleasing and attractive manner and offer so much to us as to entice, bewitch and mislead us.

There are many agencies in the world tonight that are offering people happiness, peace and rest. You are aware of them. They are publicized; they have their literature on the book stalls; they have their meetings. Some even claim to have their churches. They tell you that if you believe their message you will no longer worry, you will never again be unhappy, you will sleep perfectly, your physical illnesses may be healed and taken from you, and a thousand other things. They seem to be offering to do the very things the Bible tells us that God's way of salvation also offers to do.

The Bible knows all that, and that is why it is so careful to teach us how we can differentiate between the true and the false. And the Bible's reason for doing so is because our eternal destiny depends upon this matter. If this were the only life and the only world, perhaps it would not matter very much what it is that gives me peace, happiness and joy. If I knew for certain that when I came to die, that would be the end of me and my life, then of course the one thing that would matter would be to know how to have a good time and be happy while I am in this life.

But the Bible tells us that there is not only this life and this world; there is an eternity beyond. It tells us that our souls go on for ever and ever. In the light of that, says the Bible, you must be very careful that you really have that which is true and not the false. The problem is not merely 'How can I be right here?', but 'How can I be right there, throughout all eternity?' The issues are tremendous. This life, according to the Bible, is merely a kind of antechamber to the great eternal life that lies before us all. And therefore it tells us that we must pay deep attention to this. At all costs we must be certain that what is helping us is indeed God's method because, according to the Bible again, this is the only right method, the only true one, and everything else is of the devil.

So the whole question that arises is, how are we to discover the difference between the true and the false? As I say, the Bible answers the question like this: God's way of salvation is a whole consisting of many parts; and the way we can be quite sure that we are believing the gospel and not something that looks like the gospel is that these various parts are always present and never at any time are any of them absent. Every part is essential to the whole. Therefore, if any one of these parts is not there in whatever has offered itself to you and which you have believed, you should be highly suspicious. You have to ask yourself, 'Is this God's way of salvation?' And not only must all these parts always be present, but the order in which they come is of vital importance also.

That is the principle which is so perfectly illustrated in this paragraph and, in particular, in these verses that we are going to look at. Your soul salvation may depend upon grasping this. There are people following cults around the world who say, 'All is well' because the cult has solved their problems. But if this word is true, they are as damned and as hopeless now as they were before they went into the cult. That is why it is important for us to know how to differentiate.

We saw from verses 29 to 30 that the great characteristic of this gospel is peace and plenty, a life which is life more abundant, a life which is life indeed, and the glorious fullness, the joy, happiness and peace. But here we go on: 'Then'—when you have realized and had all that—'Then shall ye remember your own *evil ways,* and your doings that were not good, and shall lothe yourselves in your own sight for your iniquities and for your abominations.' Are you surprised at the sequence? Do you feel like saying, 'Ah, I'm not interested in that after all. You have been carrying me with this wonderful gospel, but now you are talking about loathing ourselves! We don't like it. We don't want it. Fancy bringing us down after you've raised us up!' Is that your reaction?

But this is a most important text. It is a vital statement in the whole matter of our salvation. The cults and the false gospels never say this; they even hate it. And they denounce the Bible and the gospel for saying it. That is why it is so important to know all these parts and portions to the gospel.

Take, for instance, the psychological teaching that is so popular today and which seems full of love, joy and peace and to offer us a marvellous deliverance. Put a verse like this to a psychologist and he will denounce it. He will say, 'That old gospel made people miserable. It created problems. Man is not sinful. No, no, what men need is to trust themselves, to have self-confidence. You mustn't keep them down. Encourage them to express themselves, to believe in themselves. They've got it in them. And all these things that have been called sins—they're not sins. They are natural. They've been put into us by God and they are meant to be used and to be expressed. So don't repress and keep people down.' They hate this.

All the cults and the false panaceas are in some way or another telling us to believe in ourselves, to trust to ourselves, to get out of ourselves and away from ourselves. And in this way they offer us everything that our hearts seem to be desiring. In other words, the cults and the false teachings are only interested in giving us relief, or in giving us certain benefits. They are not really interested in us in a profound manner; they just want to get rid of the pain, the agony and the trouble. They want us to be happy and enjoying ourselves. They are not interested in truth.

But the Bible always brings this in. It is in the Bible everywhere, from the very beginning to the very end. The Bible starts with repentance, and it goes on repeating it. The Bible inculcates this self-loathing—that is the term that is used here: 'you shall lothe yourselves in your own sight for your iniquities and for your abominations.' What does this word 'lothe' mean? It means hatred of that which is hateful, of that which is displeasing or offensive. It means to regard with disgust, an intense aversion. We are told here that one of the effects of the gospel is to make people look at themselves like that: to regard themselves as an abomination with an intense sense of aversion, hatefulness and disgust.

Now that is always a part of true Christianity. Unless we know something about this, it behoves us to examine the very foundations of our position. Notice that this is said after we have been told about the new heart that God will give us. He is going to take out the stony heart and give us a heart of flesh. He is going to renew our hearts. He is going to put his Spirit within us. But after all that comes this.

In other words, there is no more certain, absolute proof of the fact that we have been born again and that we have got a new heart than that we know what it is to loathe ourselves. There is no teaching in the world today that says a thing like that but the gospel. Not one.

The question then is, why should we loathe ourselves? What is it that makes us loathe ourselves? The answer is perfectly plain and simple everywhere in the Bible: it is that this way of salvation and solving our problems is one that is based upon and leads us to a knowledge of God. None of the others do that. The others start with us and they end with us. But this way is designed from beginning to end to bring us face to face with God. And whenever a man sees God, he sees himself and loathes himself.

I could illustrate this endlessly out of the Scriptures. Take the famous example of Job, who spends a lot of his time in arguing with God, grumbling and complaining, and feeling that God is not fair. At last he comes to this position. God has spoken to him and has revealed himself; he has brought his pressure to bear upon him. Listen to Job saying, 'I have heard of thee by the hearing of the ear: but now mine eye seeth thee. Wherefore I abhor myself, and repent in dust and ashes' (Job 42:5, 6). Why does he abhor himself? Because he is now face to face with God. While he was arguing with his friends he did not abhor himself. While he was arguing with God and about God he did not abhor himself. 'But now mine eye seeth thee. Wherefore I abhor myself.' He puts his hand upon his mouth.

We see the same thing in Psalm 51. David loathes himself. Why? Not simply because of what he has done, but for this reason: 'Against thee, thee only, have I sinned, and done this evil in thy sight' (Psa. 51:4).

Do you remember the man in Psalm 73 who complained so much of God's dealings with him? 'Why are the ungodly so successful? Why am I having a hard time? It isn't fair.' He is on the point of giving up and turning his back on God and all his people when he goes into the sanctuary of God. Then 'understood I their end' (verse 17): he sees God. And this is what he says: 'I was as a beast before thee' (verse 22). He abhors himself; he loathes himself.

Do you remember what happened to Isaiah when he had that vision of God? 'Woe is me!' he said. 'I am a man of unclean lips, and I dwell in the midst of a people of unclean lips' (Isa. 6:5). 'There is no health, there is no soundness. I am vile.' The moment men or women come near God, they see themselves and they loathe themselves.

Do you remember what happened to the apostle Peter? It took a good deal to bring down a self-confident, impulsive, boastful man like Peter. But remember when our Lord performed the miracle that enabled them to catch fish. Suddenly there was a revelation of his glory and his Godhead, and even Peter turned to Christ and said, 'Depart from me; for I am a sinful man, O Lord' (Luke 5:8). The presence of Christ, the manifestation of his glory, revealed to Peter his own vileness.

Our Lord put it once and for ever in the parable of the prodigal son. When the man comes to himself he says, 'Father, I have sinned against heaven, and in thy sight, and am no more worthy to be called thy son' (Luke 15:21). He was too good to be his son when he left home at the beginning, but now he is unworthy to be his son.

The apostle Paul in Romans 7 cries out in agony, saying, 'O wretched man that I am! who shall deliver me from the body of this death?' (verse 24)—this law of sin within my members, this thing that drags me down, this vileness that is within me.

Later on, in writing to Timothy and looking back across his former life, he says he was previously 'a blasphemer, and a persecutor, and injurious' (1 Tim. 1:13). How ashamed he was. How he hated it all. He loathed himself.

That is the scriptural teaching. So what is it that makes us loathe ourselves in that way? We have seen that all these men of God did so, and I trust we begin to see that if we do not know anything about this we are unlike the greatest saints the world has ever known. They say with Charles Wesley, 'Vile and full of sin I am.' Do you know anything about that? Let me give you some of the reasons why we ought to be loathing ourselves.

We should loathe ourselves first of all because of our folly. God here says through the prophet Ezekiel, 'Then shall ye remember your own evil ways, and your doings that were not good, and shall lothe yourselves.' The people did loathe themselves when they found themselves in Babylon and realized the truth. When they saw what they had been and what they had done, what fools they were, they loathed themselves. 'If only we could get back and have another chance', they said.

The same is still true today. Read the autobiography of any saint who has ever lived and you will find that they dwell on this folly. You see, when men and women become Christians and when their eyes are opened to the truth, they realize the unutterable, indescribable folly of putting their own thoughts and ideas before those of God.

There is nothing more foolish than that. Yet that is what men and women are doing by the million today. They are not interested in the Bible. Here is a book that tells us about life and how it should be lived and enjoyed, but they laugh at it; they ridicule it as being out of date and old fashioned. They dismiss it. What do they put before it? The kind of life depicted in the Sunday newspapers. That is life.

But when they become awakened and when they have a new heart, a new mind and a new understanding, they say, 'Is it credible? Could I have ever been such a fool? Could I have rejected all this, the mind of God and the exposition of eternity and time? I have rejected all that, and look what I put in its place: my thoughts and my ideas, which I couldn't even argue out. And other people could often demolish my arguments. Yet I stuck to that and rejected this.' The folly of it all!

Remember that these children of Israel had turned their backs upon God and had been worshipping idols. They had heard of other nations with their gods made of wood and stone, and they had made them and bowed down to them. But at last they had been awakened and they realized something of the truth of the sarcasm of some of those prophets who ridiculed idol worship. They said, 'Your god, he's got eyes but he can't see. He's got ears but he can't hear. He's got a nose but he can't smell. He's got legs but he can't walk. That's your god, and you have worshipped him and have turned your backs upon the living God.' Fools! It is the fool who hath said in his heart, 'There is no God.'

And again, when people come to themselves and have this enlightenment which the gospel alone can give, they see what fools they have been in taking so long to believe this gospel and to surrender themselves to it. They look back across all their clever arguments and the brilliant points that they scored, and they see that all the time they were just fooling themselves, just blinding themselves, trying to buttress up a shaky position which never had any validity at all. And they went on doing it for years. They were not honest; they were not open; they were not really listening to the message. They were simply trying to think of ways to put it down. All along they were trying to defend their own position. They talked about free will, a free mind and an open outlook. But the whole time, they see that they were governed by prejudice. And they hate and despise themselves for it.

The height of their folly is seen in this: not only have they been saying foolish and childish irrational things, but in doing so they have actually been defying God. They have been resisting him. Though they are but creatures passing through time whose lives are frail—here today and gone tomorrow—though they have no guarantee that they will be alive in a week's time, they do not hesitate to stand up and say, 'Very well, I'll defy it all. I don't care what you say. I am the master of my fate. I am the captain of my soul. I'm not bowing down to your God or to anybody else. I know. I trust my own mind and my own opinion.' They defy the God in whose hand their very breath and all their ways are; the God who made the cosmos out of nothing and could end it in a second; the God who is eternal and everlasting; the Judge of all the earth who is absolutely righteous and holy. These little pygmy creatures of time, who stand in their greatness and who can be blown to nothing in a second, defy the everlasting and eternal God.

What would you think of a person who deliberately runs to the place where an atomic bomb is to be dropped? Yet that is nothing to what men and women do when they defy God and put their little minds against the Scriptures and against the testimony of history, against the evidence of creation, against the life of the Lord Jesus Christ and his teaching, and against the Father eternal. 'Then shall ye ... lothe yourselves.' You will despise yourself for your folly, your intellectual folly, your ignorance, your arrogance and, above all, the folly of speaking at all against such a God, when the whole time you are in his hands.

I come back again to Job. The moment Job had this revelation of God, he put his hand over his mouth. It is because
people have never known God that they talk so much about
him and argue so much about him. Nothing is so enjoyable
as a religious argument. But oh, the folly of it all! I look back
across my own little life and I loathe myself for some of the
things I have said in my own cleverness.

But the second cause for loathing ourselves is that we realize our depravity. 'Then shall ye remember your own *evil
ways*, and your doings that were not good, and shall lothe
yourselves in your own sight for your iniquities and for your
abominations.'

When people have received this new heart, this new life,
this new understanding, they then look back at what they did
before. They see the things that they did, that they enjoyed,
that they put before God, that they would not give up, not
even in order to please God. They look back at these things
they thought were wonderful and say that they are evil,
iniquitous, abominable, vile, wretched, filthy, unclean.

Our blessed Lord gave a horrible list of such foul and ugly
things in Mark 7: 'For from within, out of the heart of men,
proceed evil thoughts, adulteries, fornications, murders ...'
We have the same list at the end of Romans 1: 'men with men
working that which is unseemly'; 'even their women [chang-
ing] the natural use into that which is against nature' (verses
26, 27). Oh, the foulness and the vileness and the filth of it all!
You do not need to take my word for it. Read your newspaper
every day and there you will see it. People are reading it and
they are gloating over it. They are enjoying it. They think it is
marvellous.

But when people have a new heart, they look back and they
say, 'How could I? The vileness, the foulness, the filth of it

all!' You cannot know God and see those things as you once saw them. You will hate yourself for even having looked at them.

So we loathe ourselves because of that evil nature that is within us that ever made us like those things and want them. You see, the terrible thing is not only that we have done those things and liked them; it is that there is something in us at all that ever wanted to do those things and enjoyed doing so. That is why our Lord said, 'You see, it isn't that which goes in, it's that which comes out.' There is a vileness within that expresses itself in that way. If we were pure, those things would be ugly and hateful to us. It is only because we are vile that they appeal.

There is no more terrible discovery in this world than to discover that that is the sort of nature you have; that you are twisted, unclean, so that evil, foul, iniquitous, abominable things please you. And even when you stop doing them, partly because you may be afraid, you still like reading and hearing about them. You surreptitiously borrow novels, perhaps from a library, in order to get stimulated by them. There is a craving, a desire, a fountain of evil within us all. We are all rotten: 'vile and full of sin I am.' But it is only those who have been enlightened by the Spirit of God who come to see it. The others enjoy it and defend it.

We can put it like this: it is the depravity within us that makes us antagonists of God. It is this evil within us that makes us hate the law of God and the biblical teaching about holiness. 'That Christianity of yours,' they say, 'it's so narrow, so cramped, prohibiting everything that's marvellous, tying you down, hemming you in!' Is that not the popular argument? But that is nothing but another way of saying that you hate holiness, for, judged by that criterion, the narrowest person this world has ever seen is the Lord Jesus Christ. He never did any of those things. He did not want to; they did not appeal to him. He was sorry for people who did them. That is why he sat with them and spoke to them: not to join in, but to deliver them out of it.

And when people come to realize this, they hate themselves. They loathe themselves. Why should I not desire holiness? Why should I feel that the gospel is hard? Why should I feel that God's commandments are grievous? Why should I not want to live like this and follow Christ and be like him? Why should I talk about sacrifices and about giving things up as if the gospel gave me nothing? Why is it? It is because my very nature is rotten, and I loathe myself because of it and because of my vileness.

That brings me to my third and last reason for loathing ourselves, which is our base ingratitude. 'Then shall ye remember your own evil ways, and your doings that were not good, and shall lothe yourselves in your own sight for your iniquities and for your abominations. Not for your sakes do I this, saith the Lord GOD, be it known unto you: be ashamed and confounded for your ways, O house of Israel.' What does he mean? He means that the children of Israel had been brought into being by God. He had put them in the land of Canaan, a land flowing with milk and honey. He had done it all for them, as a free gift. But they had done nothing except rebel, grumble and complain. It was all of the largesse, the munificence, the grace and the mercy of God, but they did not appreciate it. They preferred to be like the other nations and to go their own way. They spat in the face of God and upon his gifts. They despised the good land. And that is why they were in captivity. But now at last they see it: what fools they have been, how depraved they are, and the base ingratitude. They did not appreciate what God had done for them. They threw the gift back in his face.

When you realize you have done a thing like that, you feel that finally there is nothing so despicable as that. To defy the might and the power of God, as I have said, is unutterable folly, but to spurn his love is infinitely worse. There is nothing more terrible we ever do to any human individual in this life than to show a lack of appreciation for their goodness and kindness. There is nothing so terrible as to spurn love.

Yet that is precisely what all who are not Christians are doing with God. There is a sense in which I understand a person objecting to the teaching, the law and the holiness. It is totally wrong to object to it, but one can understand it. But what defies understanding is the way in which men and women can spurn and reject the love of God. 'God so loved the world, that he gave his only begotten Son, that whosoever believeth in him should not perish, but have everlasting life' (John 3:16). If God had only given the law through Moses, the Ten Commandments, the exalted teaching on holiness and no more, in a sense there might perhaps be some sort of an excuse. But God did not stop at that. 'When the fulness of the time was come, God sent forth his Son, made of a woman, made under the law' (Gal. 4:4). The babe in the manger at Bethlehem was God's only begotten Son. That babe had come out of the eternal bosom. He had left the courts of heaven and glory to be born of a woman in a stable and placed in a manger. This is God's love to men and women in sin.

God sent his only Son into the world to redeem the world. God sent him not only to teach us, to preach to us and to live before us; still more amazing and incredible is that God sent his only begotten Son into the world to die. 'God so loved the world, that he gave his only begotten Son' includes the cross.

He gave him, even unto death: 'He that spared not his own Son, but delivered him up for us all ...' (Rom. 8:32). It was God who sent him to the cross. It was God who ordained his death. It was God who gave him the commission to come and bear the sins and the guilt of men and women and receive their punishment in order that they might be forgiven. It was God who planned it; it was God who sent him; and the Son came voluntarily. That is the love of God. He punished your sins in him. He did not spare his Son anything; he kept nothing back. The last ounce was put on him and the wrath was entirely poured out upon it.

And mankind curls its lip at the cross and the blood. They ridicule it. They do not appreciate or realize what God has done. They throw it back in his face. But when they have this new heart and this new understanding and they look back upon the things they have said in their ignorance, they loathe themselves.

I once saw a man aged seventy-seven converted. There is nothing remarkable in that. Do not believe people who tell you that only young people can be converted—it is a lie. This man came to this new life and had a new heart at the age of seventy-seven. After he had joined the church, the time came for him to receive his first communion. He thought it was the greatest night of his life when took the bread and the wine to declare his Lord's death till he come. The next morning, though, before I had got up, he was at my house, brokenhearted, weeping and crying so terribly that he could scarcely be controlled. I could not understand why he was so disconsolate. Eventually, when I had controlled him, he told me: 'I shouldn't have taken that communion last night.' I said, 'Why not?' Again he could not speak and I had to control him. 'Why shouldn't you have taken it?' I asked again.

Then, in his tears and in brokenness, he said, 'Thirty years ago I was in a public house and we were arguing about God and about Jesus Christ. And I said that Jesus Christ was a bastard.' It had all come back to him. He had forgotten about it throughout the years, but now it came back and he loathed himself—so much so that he felt he did not even have a right to take communion. Thank God, I was able to explain to him that he, like Paul, had done it in ignorance, in unbelief, and that Christ died even for that sin; that even that sin had been blotted out and that, in a sense, no one had a greater right to commune than he.

When people realize that they have spurned the love of God, there is no need to argue: they must loathe themselves with an intense and bitter loathing. 'What is it in me that makes me so blind? What is it in me that's so hard? How is it that I couldn't see it?'

Do you loathe yourself? Do you know this experience? I do not care how happy you are. I do not care what peace you have. I do not care whether your body has been healed. I do not care what experience you may tell me of. Unless you know something about this self-loathing, it is not Christ who has given you peace. When he gives you these blessings, he does so in terms of bringing you to a knowledge of God and, through that, to a knowledge of yourself. And when you know yourself, you will loathe yourself with bitter loathing and hatred. You will abominate yourself. You will be disgusted with yourself. Are you?

If you are not, go to God. Flee to him and ask him by his Holy Spirit so to reveal his holiness to you that you may see yourself. Ask him by the Spirit so to reveal to you the death of Christ upon the cross as a revelation of sin, in its utter foulness, power and might, that you will loathe it within yourself.

Ask him by the Spirit so to reveal his love to you that you loathe yourself for your hard, callous and unmoved heart and spirit. Oh, give yourself no rest nor peace until by the Spirit of God you have seen yourself as you are, in sin! And that nothing but the death of Christ for you upon the cross and his rising again for your justification could ever put you right with God and save your immortal soul, and give you blessings, not only in this world and in this life, but beyond death in the presence of God through all eternity. Do it now.

12. The Temple in the Soul

Thus saith the Lord G*OD; In the day that I shall have cleansed you from all your iniquities I will also cause you to dwell in the cities, and the wastes shall be builded. And the desolate land shall be tilled, whereas it lay desolate in the sight of all that passed by. And they shall say, This land that was desolate is become like the garden of Eden; and the waste and desolate and ruined cities are become fenced, and are inhabited.*
—Ezekiel 36:33-35

I keep emphasizing how this paragraph is one of those extraordinary full views of the Christian gospel and all its benefits which we have scattered about in the Old Testament because there are still people today who seem to be so dulled by sin that they cannot see the gospel in the Old Testament. They think it is not the same God, the same covenant, the same gracious purposes, in the Old and the New Testaments. But it is the same message—it is the form alone that differs—and thus there is frequently some advantage in looking at the gospel through the Old Testament pictures. There is no doubt that men and women are helped by pictures and illustrations. We are told that that is especially true today: that people can no longer listen or read, but they like looking at things; they like pictures and illustrations. If that is so, there is a special advantage in looking at the gospel in terms of some of these

185

Old Testament pictures at this present time. And I feel that has a very particular application to this picture that we are going to look at now.

There are certain preliminary points that must of necessity strike us at once. The first is that this is yet an addition. 'Thus saith the Lord GOD; In the day that I shall have cleansed you from all your iniquities I will also ...' We have come across a number of these 'alsos'. God has said he is going to bring them back from captivity into their own land; we saw that in verse 24. Then he begins to divide it up and to put it in detail. He is going to sprinkle clean water upon them, so that they will be clean from all their filthiness and their idols. He will also give them a new heart and a new spirit. He keeps adding to it: 'And,' he says, 'also ...' Thus we are reminded of the perfection of this Christian salvation; of the endlessness of the benefits and the consequent glory of this astounding way of redemption.

As I study this paragraph and analyse it from week to week, I feel increasingly convinced that our greatest trouble is our failure to realize the greatness of God's way of redemption and salvation. I suppose this is the final sin: that we persist in measuring God by our own measures. In our foolish sinful arrogance, we measure the very being and person of God; we claim to be able to understand God and his eternal mind, and we reject the gospel because we cannot understand it. Thus all along we are trying to bring God down to our measures. And we do so with regard to the benefits of salvation.

This is something that is true not only of those who are not Christians, but also of us who are Christians. Our greatest trouble is our failure to see the glory, the greatness, the scope of it all. Part of the explanation of this curious tendency on our part is our failure to realize the nature of sin and the havoc that sin has wrought in the lives of men and women and in the world. More and more I come to see that it is a defective view of sin that accounts for the defect everywhere, because God's salvation is designed to undo all the nefarious and evil effects of sin. The first epistle of John puts it perfectly: 'For this purpose the Son of God was manifested, that he might destroy the works of the devil'—which means 'undo them, cancel them out' (1 John 3:8). Christ came into the world in order that he might entirely undo all that the devil has done to God's perfect creation and especially in the life of man.

And this paragraph is showing us how, one by one, the Lord Jesus Christ is undoing the works of the devil: by his coming into this world, by his active life of obedience, by his atoning sacrificial death when he made himself a substitute for our sins, and by his rising again from the dead and bursting asunder the bands of death and returning to the right hand of God's presence. That mighty movement of his from eternity into time and into hell and back again into glory has resulted in the works of the devil being undone and destroyed one by one. And he will complete the work. All that sin has done to this world is finally going to be removed entirely and utterly. Now, we must say with the author of the epistle of Hebrews, 'we see not yet all things put under him. But we see Jesus' (Heb. 2:8, 9). We see the process going on. It is not yet finished but is still continuing, and it will go on until it is perfectly completed. And there will be nothing left of the evil effects of sin and of Satan.

This little word 'also' reminds us of all that, almost as soon as we start our consideration of this particular statement. Among the many things that salvation gives us, the first thing is forgiveness of sins, as this verse reminds us: 'Thus saith the Lord GOD; In the day that I shall have cleansed you from all

SAVED BY GRACE ALONE

your iniquities I will also ...' Nothing will happen until he has cleansed us from our iniquities. Do not look to any blessing from God until you know that your sins are forgiven because of the shed blood of Jesus Christ. There is no relationship between man and God until man's sin has been removed. And that is how it is removed: it is God's action in Christ. 'God was in Christ, reconciling the world unto himself, not imputing their trespasses unto them' (2 Cor. 5:19). He did it like this: 'He hath made him to be sin for us, who knew no sin; that we might be made the righteousness of God in him' (5:21). And following this blotting out of our transgressions come all the other things we have been considering: the new heart, the new mind, the Spirit of God coming within, the promise that we shall be his people and he will be our God, the abundance of blessings; and then the way in which anyone who realizes all God's munificence loathes himself for his vileness and stupidity in standing against such a God and rejecting such a wondrous offer.

But it does not stop even at that: there is more. As we look at it, we are once more reminded of the principle that everything about God's salvation is the exact opposite of what people think it to be. There is no better proof than that of the fact that the god of this world has blinded the minds of those who do not believe. For example, here is a great promise that the redeemed shall live together in cities: 'Thus saith the Lord GOD; In the day that I shall have cleansed you from all your iniquities I will also cause you to dwell in the cities, and the wastes shall be builded.' And at the end he summarizes by putting it like this: 'and the waste and desolate and ruined cities are become fenced, and are inhabited.' That is the exact opposite of what mankind in its blindness and ignorance generally thinks about this gospel.

The Temple in the Soul

If you are Christian, go back in your mind to a time when you were not Christian, and I think you will find this (and if you are not Christian you will confirm it now): we all by nature seem to have the idea that to become a Christian is somehow to isolate ourselves. We think of it as a great giving up and going out of. There is the wonderful world, with all its company, happiness, joy and camaraderie, and you are to become a Christian. And what does that mean? It means stepping out from the crowd on your own and becoming a lonely pilgrim in some sort of wilderness, isolated and alone.

That was part of the trouble of the rich young ruler in Luke 18. So much to give up! He was going to be stripped, to become helpless, to be desolate; he was not going to have anything at all! He was going to be absolutely on his own and isolated! And he shrank from it and went away sorrowful.

That idea seems to have been in Peter's mind when he said, 'You know, we have given up homes and houses, such an awful lot.' And he seems to ask by implication, 'What have we got?' (Mark 10:28). That is how the world always thinks of Christianity: it is something that leads people to isolation, loneliness, a kind of wilderness existence by contrast with the great fellowship of the life that is apart from God.

The second way in which this misunderstanding tends to manifest itself is that people seem to think that the Christian faith is entirely opposed to what they call 'civilization'. They are constantly putting up the message about civilization against the Christian message. You find that running right through the Bible and through history everywhere. What man opposes to God's way is what he calls his own civilization and all that that represents in his mind. He means that this is a kind of organized life of men. He thinks that Christianity is that which keeps man in a primitive condition, uncultured,

189

unintelligent, untutored, missing all that is really of value. But, on the other hand, that which brings out the innate greatness of man is civilization. And how do you get civilization? The first thing you do is, of course, to turn your back on Christianity. Sophistication is the opposite of salvation and of Christianity. The sophisticated man, the man of culture, the man about town, the man who really is interested in being a civilized person, regards Christianity as something rather primitive, coarse and lacking in refinement.

Our text, in displaying the wonders of salvation, once more gives the lie to all such ideas and arguments. It shows us that there is nothing that finally gives us fellowship as the gospel does. And there is nothing which helps us to see ourselves and the whole of life in terms of a people, of a civilization, if you like, so much as the Christian message and the Christian faith.

Now Ezekiel here puts that in terms of two pictures. Two things are going to happen: the cities that have been desolate and in a state of ruin are going to be rebuilt and re-inhabited; and the land that was desolate, uncultivated and unfruitful is again to be brought into cultivation and is going to yield magnificent crops.

We will look only at this first picture here. It is a very common picture in the Scriptures, one used by several of the prophets. It is a picture that very naturally suggests itself because it first of all corresponds to the actual history of the people of Israel themselves. It is, therefore, a wonderful picture of what God does for mankind in Christ in a spiritual sense.

This picture has also been used by writers concerning the Christian life. John Bunyan takes up this whole idea of the heavenly warfare, this fight of faith, in his writing about the city of Mansoul in *The Holy War*. You find it in a sense in *The City of God*, that great idea of Augustine: there are these two cities, man's city—civilization so called—and the city of God.

Let us use this picture in a very simple way. What are we told here? It is the same thing that we have been told in every single step. We see first of all what sin does, and then we see what the gospel of salvation does. What does sin do? The first thing is that sin ruins life. Sin always leads to ruination and desolation. That is the great message of the Bible. It starts back in the garden of Eden, where it began. Man and woman started in paradise, but they are no longer there. Their world is no longer paradise but desolation. This is always the story.

But the prophet no doubt had primarily the actual history of the children of Israel in his mind. God had given them the land and there they had built their great city of Jerusalem, which was the pride of the country: the great city set upon a high elevation, a majestic city, the Mecca of all the people, the place to which they went and in which they took such great pride. But now, when Ezekiel wrote, these people were captives in the land of Babylon, far away from their own country and from Jerusalem.

Before the enemy that defeated them carried them away as captives to Babylon, he first of all had attacked, sacked and destroyed the city of Jerusalem and other cities. So when these people were carried away, it is a literal truth to say that their cities were in ruin and desolate. The great buildings had come crashing to the ground. That is a fact of history.

The Bible takes up that idea and uses it as a wonderful picture. We look at man, if you like, as a kind of city of God. We can look at God's people in the same way. What do we see? We see that magnificent city set upon a hill, the pride and joy of the people. We see the magnificent wall round it. We see the turrets and the battlements, the towers built for the defence of the city so that no marauders, no enemies, might suddenly steal into the city, kill the people and take their goods and possessions. What a wonderful city it is! What a glorious prospect! Do you see certain great buildings standing out: magnificent palaces, great museums, noble structures with works of art, places of culture and interest? And then, above them all and more important than them all, there is a temple, the place where the people went to meet God, the place that linked them to heaven, the place in which they were given assurance that their sins were again covered and that God was looking upon them with benignity; the temple, the ultimate pride of the people, the sanctuary of God, the meeting place of heaven and earth. There is your great city. And the life of the city is an ordered and disciplined life, a life of fellowship amongst the people. And the people were all together in their city, which they called the city of God.

But, alas, they had become negligent. Because of their forgetfulness of God and their sin, they had not seen to the repairs of the wall. It was just simple neglect; they had no time for it, they were busy with other things, living for the moment, forgetting the enemy, forgetting everything except the immediate enjoyment of the moment. They had become neglectful of the walls and the defences. As a result, the day arrived when a powerful enemy came and made breaches through these weak points in the wall. And there the enemy began pouring into the city. And he razed these mighty buildings to the ground. He sacked the temple; he desecrated it. He took away the very vessels, the ornaments, the gold and the silver, and he left it a mass of rubble, a wretched, desolate ruin.

That is the picture. The prophet is not exaggerating; he is actually giving us sheer facts.

That is what the enemy did to the city of Jerusalem. And here are the people, away in captivity, and they think of their own land and they see it untilled and as a mass of ruin and rubble, no longer inhabited, and themselves scattered abroad as captives.

That is a perfect account in pictorial form of what sin does to man. Man can be thought of in these terms. What a piece of work is man! Oh, how wonderfully has God made us! These various buildings to which I have been alluding refer to the mind, the understanding, the ability. I have talked about the museums and the places of art, man's conscionable ability. They are given by God. Man has not created these things. Shakespeare did not make Shakespeare, nor was he responsible for Shakespeare. Every gift that any man or woman has is God-given. A person is born a musician, a poet or an artist. These gifts are all given by God, implanted within us. There are some magnificent buildings in the city—great palaces, the place of morality, the place of government, the civic centre, the town hall; there is order, arrangement, government. God made man like that. He gave him a balanced life: body, soul and spirit. All these parts and all these magnificent gifts were there.

More important than them all is the temple, that in man which is made for God and where God meets with man. God made man in his own image and he made him for himself. And he made this possibility of communion. There is a temple in the soul, in the heart, of every living being. It was placed there by God and it was meant for God. It is there we meet with God, the temple. And God gave originally to man the possibility of not sinning—the defence.

So there is man in the world. But, alas, man is no longer like that. Sin has come in, and sin always leads to ruin, chaos and desolation. Notice the terms that are used in our text: 'In the day that I shall have cleansed you from all your iniquities I will also cause you to dwell in the cities, and the *wastes* shall be builded.' Then we read these words: 'and the *waste* and the desolate and *ruined* cities are become fenced, and are inhabited.' But, at the time of writing, they were not like that; they were in the exact opposite position.

What is it that sin does to man? It is just a repetition of this sad and sorry story that happened to the children of Israel. First of all there is a breach in the wall and in the defence. The enemy always starts with that. I do not believe in the Peter Pan conception of man in life and in this world, but there is a sense in which we are innocent and start like that. But a day comes in our history when, because of our neglect of these things, because of forgetfulness of God and our failure to apply teaching, and because of the whole subtlety and insinuation of Satan and of sin, an attack is made, a breach is made in the wall and an enemy enters in. The defences are no longer intact. We begin to yield to sin. It becomes enticing and attractive. And we allow an enemy in.

Then the enemy proceeds with his methods. The law and order that characterizes the life of a city is the next thing he always attacks. He attacks the discipline of our lives. Discipline becomes slacker and slacker. 'Of course,' we say, 'when we were children, we took these things desperately seriously. But that was ignorance; we know now.' 'What is there wrong in this one glass? Surely there is no harm in one glass — that can never lead to trouble?' Already the discipline is beginning to shake. That first one leads to the final one and the gutter.

And then the enemy begins to attack some of those magnificent buildings, man's moral greatness and grandeur. Oh, how the enemy is attacking that at the present time! Indeed, this building has obviously been razed to the ground. People no longer seem to believe in morality. They do not recognize it as a category. 'There's nothing wrong in it,' they say. 'What are you talking about?' Some of the most offensive forms of evil are being portrayed as very beautiful and wonderful.

There was a time not very long ago when in public appointments and even membership of Parliament there were certain things that excluded people. They no longer exclude them now. The whole moral conception of man has been shaken to its foundations. It has come crashing down. We do not know where we are morally in this modern world. That magnificent building has been brought down by the enemy.

And as a more or less direct consequence, some of the other great and most glorious buildings have come crashing down also. Is there not a general lowering of the manifestation of the highest powers of man? For example, we seem to have lost our ideas as to what constitutes music. Melody is despised and cacophony is gloried in. To be melodious is to be hum-drum, to be Victorian. A clash of discords is regarded as wonderful. And people spend their time listening to that which comes from primitive peoples. There is no mind there; it is mere rhythm, mere animal, mere appeal to the sensibilities. There is no thought, nothing uplifting, nothing ennobling. You just sit down like savages and are moved mechanically.

Though we boast of our education, culture and advance, that is what is happening in life. These gorgeous buildings, these magnificent edifices, have been sacked and ruined by the enemy. And we are going back to a primitive kind of state of existence.

And above all, of course, the temple has been sacked and left a mass of rubble. Is there still a temple in your life? Is there still a sanctuary of God in your soul? Do you meet with God when you are alone? To put the question of a recent philosopher, what do you do with your own solitude? He said, 'That's religion: what a man does with his own solitude.'[1] What do you do with your own solitude? Do you meet with God in the temple of your soul? Is it there? Is it still standing?

What about the other buildings? What of your morality? Your chastity? To what use are you putting the gifts that God has given you? What of these glorious buildings with which God originally endowed men; are they standing? What of the wall, the battlements, the towers? Are there breaches? Is the wall standing or is it down? Has the enemy come flooding into your life? Do you know where you are? Are you in control? Is there any government, order and discipline, or is all chaos, wilderness, confusion and ruin?

Is it not obvious today that this is what sin does to man? And man, as I said at the beginning, seems to think that if you want to have a happy life of community and fellowship, you must never become a Christian because that leads to isolation and solitude. He thinks that it is with the world and the crowd that you can have fellowship. But is it not a simple truth that life is becoming increasingly lonely? We read of that in the papers, and we find it in actual practice. Life is becoming more and more lonely. There is no place on earth which is so lonely, in a sense, as a great city. You stand on a corner and you see people rushing hither and thither. They are all of them passing you by and you stand alone.

[1] See Alfred N. Whitehead, *Religion in the Making, Lowell Lectures 1926* (New York: Fordham University Press, 1926).

This problem is becoming a very urgent one with regard to the elderly and those who are sick. A hundred years ago, when this country was much more Christian than it is today, there was much more fellowship. I remember how, when someone was taken ill in the little community in which I had the privilege of being brought up, it didn't matter who the person was: everybody went there. One took a dinner, another took a tea, yet another took money. We all tried to do something. We were all one. But I am told it is no longer like that. Everyone has to fend for himself. People have not got time to go and sit an evening with a sick elderly person. They must run to their form of entertainment. They have this engagement or they are looking at that. Lonely people are increasing in numbers, but they are left to themselves. No one seems to think about them. What to do with lonely sick and elderly people is an acute problem in the life of this country. In this age in which we are all supposed to be one and we are talking about our common life, helping one another and all being looked after by the state, loneliness is becoming a great problem.

It is desolation; it does not give you a life of fellowship. It is the sinful life that leads you to isolation and you are left alone, like the prodigal in the far country, down and out, and no one interested. When they saw him coming, they said, 'I'll walk the other way. That fellow's coming to beg again.' Selfishness, self-centredness, all out for themselves: that is the life of sin. There is no fellowship, no community; rather the exact opposite.

Thank God for a gospel that undoes that kind of thing! There is nothing else that can do it but the gospel. It is God who does this, as he does everything else: 'I will also cause you to dwell in the cities.' They could not do it themselves in Babylon, could they? There was no point in trying to call

a meeting together of the exiles in Babylon and to talk about
their land and their city. They did not have any arms. They
were in the hands of a cruel oppressor and they were small in
number. They could do nothing. They could not get together
and say, 'We'll go back and rebuild': that was impossible.
But God could and God did. God could influence the mind
and heart of a pagan ruler for the sake of his own people. He
could put them back, build the cities, inhabit them and put
them back in the position where they were before. And that is
what happened historically. And it happens equally gloriously
in a spiritual sense as the result of the salvation that we have
in Jesus Christ our Lord.

Do you remember the man in the hymn who prays like this:

> The ruins of my soul repair
> And make my heart a house of prayer?

A man who offers that prayer from his heart will find it
answered in Christ. What does he do? He starts by clearing
away the rubbish and the rubble. And what a lot of it there
is: the rubbish and rubble of our own foolish philosophies,
our own clever ideas and thoughts. There will be an awful lot
of rubble to clear away as the result of this present modern
civilization. It is making a terrible havoc in life. You see it in
the newspapers and in the reports of the courts. It is all to be
swept away and cleared so that the site can again be made
free.

And when the Holy Spirit gets to work, he does it; he clears
it away. This is an astounding thing. He can clear it away in
a second. You can tenaciously hold onto your own opinions
and ideas. But then, in a moment, you suddenly find they
have all gone! That is what happened to Saul of Tarsus on
the road to Damascus. He went breathing out threatenings

and slaughter: confident, self-assured, absolutely determined that Christ was an impostor and that this Christianity was the last height of folly, and determined to exterminate it. And yet in a second he cried out, 'What wilt thou have me to do, Lord?' The rubble and the rubbish had all been cleared away. The site was free.

We preach a miraculous salvation. It is not the slow process of teaching and instruction. It is not like going to a school or university and learning a little bit more every day. There may be no time for that. No, the Holy Spirit can do it in a flash, in a second. It is his miraculous work.

What does he do then? He brings out the new plans and the new specifications and he begins to measure it out, order it and arrange it. And you begin to see the possibilities of a new tidiness in your life. A city shall be rebuilt. And however bad cities may become, there is always a certain order, form and tidiness about the life of a city. And that is what the gospel of Jesus Christ does in a person's life. Into the chaos and the unutterable confusion that sin makes, he comes and brings order. He makes you see life in a simple manner, in a new way. Now there are only certain big things that count. You are no longer pulled by this temptation, attracted and enticed by that lust. You are no longer at the mercy of all these forces; you have got a simple plan of life. This is a wonderful aspect of the gospel: it simplifies the whole of existence. There is a plan and a purpose. You begin to see yourself again as a pilgrim of eternity. You see that this is a passing, temporary world. You begin to have your eye on eternity, and you see that you were made for God and that the great thing is to be right with him. Your whole life is reduced to a plan.

This is a wonderful thing! You feel that you are in the hands of the eternal Architect and that he really is going to rebuild. Of course it is a process. Having laid the foundation in the rebirth and regeneration, he goes on building. And the buildings go up, one after another. It is marvellous to be conscious of this. An interest in the Bible, an interest in prayer: buildings are going up that were not there before. But now I can enter that building and there I read and there my mind expands. Here I turn into another building: I am now interested in morality. I am interested in growing in grace and in the knowledge of the Lord. I am interested in being free from sin and in living a holy life like Christ. What a pattern! I look at the picture and I gaze in amazement and astonishment.

And I begin to enjoy prayers. I like turning into the temple; I go there more and more. There was a time when I did not; it was not there. But it is being rebuilt and I go and meet God. And just to complete my picture, the government and the discipline, the central authority, is there once more—the bylaws. I become interested in them. They are no longer dull and boring. I see they are all designed for me and for my benefit. I used to rebel against this sort of thing and I wanted my own way, to be absolutely free. I did not care about my neighbour. But I see now that life in community must be ordered. 'Look not every man on his own things, but every man also on the things of others. Let this mind be in you, which was also in Christ Jesus' (Phil. 2:4, 5). This is a life of order, central government and authority.

I close with the most marvellous thing of all: the fellowship. There is nothing more wonderful about the Christian life than this. You suddenly discover that it is not the isolated life you thought it was. For the first time in your life you really discover friends; you discover brothers and sisters. We must be quite clear about this. When you become a Christian, you may at first have that awful feeling that you are going to stand absolutely alone. You may be the only member of your family who is a Christian, and because you have become a Christian there is a separation between you and the others. They are all still one with the same interests; you are the isolated one, alone. And the devil comes and tells you, 'Well, now you've done it. You are going to spend your life in lonely misery.'

But it is not true. Listen to the words of our Lord Jesus Christ:

> Peter began to say unto him, Lo, we have left all, and have followed thee. And Jesus answered and said, Verily I say unto you, There is no man that hath left house, or brethren, or sisters, or father, or mother, or wife, or children, or lands, for my sake and the gospel's, but he shall receive an hundredfold now in this time, houses, and brethren, and sisters, and mothers, and children, and lands, with persecutions; and in the world to come eternal life.' (Mark 10:28-30)

It is absolutely true. I remember once having to take the funeral service of a man who was a member of the church where I was privileged to minister in South Wales. He died at an old age and he had no relatives at all. We could not trace any anywhere. He did not know whether any were alive anywhere or not. You would have thought, 'There is a man who is absolutely isolated.' In that town they still had old-fashioned funerals, and it was the custom for the relatives always to walk immediately behind the coffin in the procession; other members of the public walked in front. So we all felt there was only one thing to do. We were all the relatives. So the entire church walked behind the coffin. Of course we did: he was my brother; the women Christians felt that he was their brother. We were all related. We were all one. We are members of the family of God. We enter into a great and glorious fellowship.

We become a people. We have the same interests, the same happiness. We share the same experiences. We enjoy the same blessings together.

I have often said this in my vestry to kind friends who come here as visitors in the summer from other lands. As I shake their hands and look at them I feel that I have known them all my life. I can tell by looking at them that they are Christians. And we feel we belong to one another.

In the war, with troops here from different countries, it was marvellous that they would come and speak to me, and I felt it was an absolute proof that God's family is one throughout the whole world. Isolation? No, it is the sinful life that leaves you alone. Here, you come into a community and into a family: children of God, heirs of God and joint heirs with Christ, participators together in the common salvation.

And beyond this life and this world is that glorious prospect which is described in Revelation 7: that vast multitude so great that it cannot be counted; thousands upon thousands, all together in their white robes. Who are they? They are God's people. They are all one. They are children of their heavenly Father. And they are going to enjoy and spend their eternity together. But outside are those living the old selfish, self-centred, aggressive, quarrelling, disputing, hateful, hidden life. No community; that is hell. Hell is every man for himself, and all against each other and against God, for ever and ever without relief. How terrible.

But in heaven, they mingle their voices in singing the same anthem, praising the same God and worshipping the same Lamb who was slain for their sins and who has redeemed them unto God. Oh, the fellowship! The city of God descends and we shall be in it and spend eternity there. This is the life of community, the life of oneness and of unity in God.

Sin makes desolate, ruins and separates. The gospel builds, establishes, unites, and gives us a fellowship with God and with his Son, Jesus Christ, and with one another. Thank God for a gospel that undoes the effects of sin from beginning to end, and that will ultimately present us faultless and blameless in the presence of God, all one in Christ and spending our eternity together.

13. The Unproductive Age

*And the desolate land shall be tilled, whereas it lay desolate
in the sight of all that passed by. And they shall say, This land
that was desolate is become like the garden of Eden.*
                                        —Ezekiel 36:34, 35

THERE is no more glorious statement of the benefits of
salvation which is to be obtained in Jesus Christ our Lord
than that which we have in this paragraph, and here is yet
another addition. There is literally no end to the blessings of
salvation. Paul refers to them as 'the exceeding riches of his
grace' (Eph. 2:7). You cannot describe them. They are so marvellous; they are endless. But it is our business to look at the
details that we are given.

Now we remember the principle that the business of the
gospel is to undo the effects of sin. We previously looked at
what we called the *ruinous* effects of sin. Our theme was that
sin is that which ruins life. It ruins man; it ruins the soul; it
defaces God's image in man. But here we have something further. Sin not only ruins life; it also wastes life. Sin is entirely
unproductive. It is not so much that it brings down and ruins as
that it leaves something which ought to be productive in a non-
or unproductive condition, and that is nothing but sheer waste.

Our text is speaking literally about the condition of the
children of Israel. Because they had been carried away captive

from their own land to Babylon, their land was not being cultivated. It was untilled; it was lying fallow, unused. There were no crops. It was derelict and desolate. That is what sin always leads to.

Are we not already reminded once again of what is the very essence of the biblical message from beginning to end: that sin is most terrible and devastating? The fall was the greatest calamity that could possibly have happened to man and to this world. If we do not agree with that, we will never understand the Christian message of salvation.

There is nothing which is quite so fatal as to think of sin as something light or, as so many do today, as something negative. Most people hate Christianity because of its doctrine of sin. They want to be cheerful and happy, and they say it is a false psychology. It has held people down. They say mankind is not like that after all. They hate the doctrine of sin today. And that is why they are not Christian.

But the biblical doctrine of sin is here from beginning to end. And it is that sin is not something light, something merely negative; it is that sin is so devastating that nothing in man has been left unaffected by it.

I wonder if we realize that. There is nothing in us but that it was affected by the fall. The fall of man and woman into sin affected their minds, their emotions, their wills. It affected every part of man: the intellectual part, the moral part, the volitional part. Divide man up as you like; there is not a part that has not been affected. When Adam and Eve fell, they fell completely. And it is a most horrible ruin, an utter desolation. These steps that we are going through one by one in this section remind us of that. They bring out the point that sin was a terrible and fearful calamity. That is the whole explanation of the state of the world today. In the newspapers and when we listen to the news, we see some of the effects and the results of the fall of man and woman and of sin. It is a calamity of the deepest type.

But—and this is the message of the gospel—however profound may be the effect of sin and the fall, the effects of the gospel are equally profound. That is why, as I bring out step by step and stage by stage the effects of the fall and of sin, I am showing you at the same time the effects of the gospel of redemption. And the gospel more than cancels out everything that the Fall and sin have done.

The apostle Paul put that in this phrase: 'where sin abounded, grace did much more abound' (Rom. 5:20). That is what I keep seeing in this paragraph. I see sin abounding. I see what it has done to man. I see the ruin, the havoc and the desolation. But then I listen to the word of God that came to the prophet Ezekiel, telling him what he was going to do. And as I listen to it, I say, 'Yes, it's all right. Sin has abounded, but grace has much more abounded.' Oh, the glories of the gospel! But you will never see them unless you first see all the devastating effects of sin.

So sin, as I said, is that which is utterly unproductive. It is barren, sterile. And I want to show you that in general and in particular. It has this effect upon the individual, upon us personally, in particular. But sin has this effect first of all in general, in the world at large. And I must point out the general because the world as it is today is a clear confirmation of this biblical message. We are living in a barren age. It is an unproductive age, whichever department of life you look at. Is that not true in the realm of music? Is it not true in the realm of art? Do you think much modern music is going to endure? Do you think people will still be trying to sing it or to listen to its being played in a hundred years' time, if there is still a world in a hundred years' time? I doubt it. How much modern poetry is going to live? It is certainly a clever age, and what you see in the music, the poetry and the art is cleverness rather than true art. You see the artifice rather than the art; the artefact rather than true artistry.

You can see this very clearly if you take a broad view of history. There have been certain eras in the history of the world when man's relationship to God has been the chief thing, the controlling factor in the life of man. These are the so-called 'ages of faith', when the Christian faith and message has counted and been supreme. You will invariably find that in all such ages of faith there has been an amazing stimulus all along the line in almost every respect. You find great architecture, great sculpture, great music, great poetry, great drama, and so on. And this is something which is actually acknowledged by many historians who are not Christians themselves. They have to admit the fact: the ages of faith have been productive. There is something about this Christian message when it influences men and women which even influences those who are not actually Christians themselves. The whole community derives a benefit.

The whole country derives a benefit when there has been a religious awakening. That is a fact. That is why the Elizabethan period, the Puritan era and the period following the great Evangelical Awakening of the eighteenth century saw some of the greatest cultural advances that this country has ever known.

But, on the other hand, the ages of unbelief have always been barren and sterile. This is a wonderful proof of the fact that man was made for God: when man is not functioning in relationship to God and as God meant him to, he fails all along the line. For example, take the period following the

Puritan era: the restoration of Charles II and all the licentiousness of his court. Men and women turned their backs upon the faith and lived according to their own ideas. It was a terribly barren period in every respect, even in a secular sense, from 1660 to about 1740.

Alas, we seem to be living in a similar age. When we contrast the productivity of this century with last century, I think every thinking person who is not hopelessly prejudiced and blinded has got to admit that we are utterly unproductive, especially if we contrast ourselves with some of those great epochs and eras. Sin is unproductive. The whole of life seems to come to a standstill.

Look at the most backward countries in the world today. You will find that they are countries where the Christian faith in its purity has been preached least. On the contrary, wherever the Christian message goes, it always provides a kind of civilization. It gives an impetus to everything that is uplifting and ennobling in the life of man. With it come education, hospitals and other improvements. The most backward peoples and races are those that have not received the powerful direct message of the Christian faith. They are backward in every respect. Here is a great confirmation of what we are told in our text.

That is the general aspect, but let us look at it in particular. After all, this applies to us individually. We will not be examined at the final bar of judgment upon the state of civilization, but upon our own condition. Yes, it is important that we should realize it works all along the line, but it is vitally urgent that we should realize it about ourselves. Therefore the question we must ask ourselves is: what is my condition today? What is the state of my soul? God made man, breathed into him the breath of life, and man became a living soul.

There is the soil, the possibility. What has happened to it? What has become of it? If we were inspected as a man might inspect a farm or an estate, what would he find? What is our productivity?

The biblical message is that sin is always unproductive and always leads to barrenness and to a sterile condition. So the life of every individual in sin is like that land of Israel when the children of Israel were in Babylon and were unable to cultivate it.

Now let me prove my point. I do so first of all in general by putting it in the form of a principle: sin must be unproductive because it never makes the right use of our faculties and therefore never draws out the possibilities that are innate and inherent within us. Sin is that which neglects the soil of the soul.

There was nobody to till the land of Israel, therefore it was unproductive. And in a state of sin, man is exactly like that. For all that sin does to us, it does not use our faculties as they should be used and therefore it does not draw out the power that is in them. Let me give you some illustrations to show what I mean. I make no apology for being very blunt, direct and practical. The newspapers and films are full of this sort of thing, so let me show you the relevance and the practical character of the preaching of the gospel.

I start with sex. The world is mad on sex; there is no question about that. This is a sex-ridden, sex-mad generation. Sex is an instinct placed in us by God, one of the faculties that God has put into men and women. But sin, instead of using sex as it was meant to be used, as a means to an end, isolates it, making it an end in itself. That is lust. The whole tragedy of people at the present time is that instead of allowing this instinct of sex to play its rightful part, it is made into headlines, it is underlined and splashed in front of us. It is taken right out of its context and regarded as an end and an object in and of itself. And people live for sex.

That is why it is unproductive. As we are told in the book of Genesis—and it is repeated in many places—sex was put into man in order that man might replenish the earth. People are not interested in replenishing the earth today. Their interest in sex is as an experience, a form of enjoyment. It is isolated and exaggerated hopelessly. And the result is barrenness and sterility, physically literally as well as spiritually.

This particular aspect of sex and of sin may very well profoundly affect the whole future of this country and the whole world. The whole balance of population may become such that what we have boasted of as our Western civilization may be entirely overcome, merely because of lack of numbers.

But let me take another illustration. Man in sin does exactly the same thing with happiness and joy: he makes them ends in themselves. But they were never meant to be that. Happiness is not an end; it is a by-product, something that is to happen more or less unconsciously because we are obeying certain laws. It was never meant to be a direct objective. But again we have isolated this and exaggerated it.

And what is work according to the modern man in sin? It is a nuisance, just something that you need to do if you want to have money to have your pleasure and happiness. Work is something hateful, abominable, and man would be delighted if something could be invented to put an end to it. It is something one has to go through in order to achieve something else. Our eye is on the pleasure, not on the dignity, the greatness, the nobility and the value of work. In other words, our whole idea is unproductive, and the end is lack of production.

But that is how sin works: it takes things which are given by God and which are right and normal, and it takes them out of their context, exaggerates and isolates them. It puts them up as the ultimate target, which they are never meant to be. And then it presses us after them. And thus we find ourselves exhausted and utterly unproductive.

Now I have been looking at this matter philosophically, or psychologically. But let me take it in the form of particular illustrations of some of the things that are most prominent in the life of modern man, things that the average individual is living for today and that are acclaimed and praised in the newspapers.

There is the question of drink. From all the talk, you would think there was nothing more marvellous in the world than the life of the local public house. How it is praised and lauded! And what a contrast it presents to a chapel or a prayer meeting!

What does drink do? Speaking strictly scientifically, from the pharmacological standpoint, the final thing to say about drink is that it is totally unproductive. What it really does is to paralyse the faculties, not to stimulate them.

Perhaps you thought drink was a stimulant; but it is not. Alcohol is a depressant. It paralyses the higher centres, the control, the balance, and as a result the more primitive things come to the surface. The man appears to be brilliant, but what is really happening is that he is beginning to be reckless. He is losing his judgment and his balance. Drink attacks the faculties; it does not draw them out or stimulate them.

Of course, something very similar is true of drugs. All drugs either overstimulate or paralyse and depress. The result is that none of our faculties are being used. They are lying waste; they are unproductive.

Or take the most obvious illustration of all, because it is one of the most popular things today: gambling. (Notice that I am not preaching against these things; I am just showing their real nature. The function of preaching is to open people's eyes to the facts about what they are doing. Then, having seen it by the Spirit, they will stop doing it.) The whole point about gambling is of course that it is entirely non-productive; it is the desire to have wealth, not because a man has worked and has achieved it and has a right to it, but simply wealth in and of itself. There is no production, nothing to show for it, no value to the community at large.

That is the principle in general. Of course, the effects of all this show themselves, as they did in the case of the land of Israel. The first thing we notice is that the effect of sin is always this lack of cultivation: that the land has an ugly, untidy appearance. If you neglect your garden for a few years, it will soon begin to look untidy. But life has become ugly and untidy, and even in such matters as personal appearance. We seem to have lost all ideas of real charm, beauty and the whole art of concealment. Life has become loud, ugly and untidy. You see it on the streets and in the newspapers.

But what is more important is that there is no crop. There is nothing to put in the barns. In other words, there is nothing in that sinful life that ennobles the soul. There is nothing that draws out and develops the faculties and increases them. There is nothing to show at the end of a long life. The apostle Paul has put this in what always seems to me the most perfect and devastating way in Romans 6: 'What fruit had ye then in those things whereof ye are now ashamed? for the end of those things is death' (verse 21). Sin is always utterly unproductive.

There is something rather terrible and awful, as well as pathetic and tragic, in the end of the life of a man who has had no use for God, who does not know him and who is not a Christian. What sorry, tragic figures are some of these brilliant, sophisticated men and women when they go out of life. You cannot help feeling sorry for them. They have entertained, amused or tickled the fancy of people. But when you look at them in their old age, they have nothing to be proud of, nothing to show, nothing that gives them satisfaction. They sit and look back upon the scenes of their former triumphs—how wonderful it was while they were yet young!—but they have nothing now. They have to skip back across the years to try to find something to give them a sense of satisfaction.

We have seen this ourselves, have we not? We may have known it personally. The sinful life is all right until something goes wrong: as long as you are well, hale and hearty, and have got money and can do your work. But suddenly you are taken ill, and the very bottom drops out of your life. You do not know where you are. You have got nothing to fall back upon, no comfort, nothing at all. You are simply left to yourself. It is utterly unproductive. There is no comfort in that life. There is nothing to lean upon. There is nothing to give you pleasure, nothing to sustain the soul. You want food at this point, spiritual food, in your loneliness when you cannot go with your boon companions or do the things you have always done. You do not know how to spend your time, how to while away the weary hours. Oh, how unproductive, barren and sterile is a life of sin!

And that is the tragedy of so many in the world today. 'Without a hope to cheer the tomb', says a line in a hymn. Is it not true? That is the point at which you test life: when you are dying and you are going out of it. You have lived your whole life: what have you got to show for it? What about the barns? What about the crops? What about the yield when the final reckoning is made? When the final auditor comes in and looks across the books of your life, what does he find? What is the productivity? The tragedy of a man or woman who has lived without God and without Christ is that they begin to realize at that point that they have got nothing at all. They do not have a character; they have lost it. They do not have a comfort, a cheer, a hope or a prospect. They have got nothing. Their faculties are exhausted and wearied. They are coming to an end and they are empty-handed. Sin is utterly unproductive.

But there is something worse than that. Not only did that land of Israel that was not being cultivated not produce crops, but it actually produced something else instead. Again, go and look at the garden which is not being cultivated. What happens? Weeds begin to grow: briars, thorns and thistles, weeds that are useless, valueless, poisonous and of no use to anybody. They spring up in abundance. And this is the tragedy of a person in sin. Not only have they got nothing ennobling, uplifting and of value to look at, to comfort themselves and to pass on to others, but the soil of their soul is full of weeds, thorns, briars and thistles. Sin always produces a crop—of misery, shame, remorse and vain regrets. Sin invariably produces suffering.

You cannot sin without suffering following. You will suffer personally. You may suffer in your health. The man who was so happy last night was terribly miserable this morning with his splitting headache and his stomach upside down, as it were, in agony, revolted. He is paying for it. There is always a crop that follows sin, and this crop is partly suffering. And it also produces suffering in others: the wife of the helpless, hopeless drunkard, and the little children; the innocent victims of divorce, the children who have done nothing to anybody.

Oh, the appalling crop of suffering that sin is producing in this modern world of ours!

And then it introduces confusion. You cannot see where the paths are in that uncultivated garden full of weeds; you cannot see where the plots were that used to produce a yield. Everything is mixed up and in a state of terrible confusion.

And then think of the crop of lying, dishonesty and deceit that always result from sin, as it did in the garden of Eden and has done ever since, to cover it over, to pretend that you have not been seen and that you have not done it. And then there is all the bitterness and the quarrels that follow.

There is still one final thing that I must say. It is a most astonishing thing, and I speak strictly accurately in terms of agriculture and horticulture: did you know that a land like that, which is uncultivated and which produces these weeds, is actually poisoned itself by these other crops that it produces? It becomes bitter, sour. It becomes so poisoned that, in a sense, it cannot produce a good crop as it is. And that is what sin always does to a man or woman. It exhausts them, poisons them. It perverts all their faculties so that they no longer can do what they were meant to do. And their whole spirit is soured, embittered and rendered sterile as the result of sin. That is what I meant when I said that all these ages of sin are always ages of barrenness and sterility. All the highest faculties in men and women are put out of commission.

That is the effect of sin. But thank God for this message of salvation: 'And the desolate land shall be tilled, whereas it lay desolate in the sight of all that passed by. And they shall say, This land that was desolate is become like the garden of Eden.' What a transformation! Do you know how it happens? It is all the result of the coming, the life, the death and the resurrection of the Lord Jesus Christ, as that is applied to the soul by the Holy Spirit. What have you got to do to this land before it can become productive again? You have got to start by clearing it up. You have got to get rid of the weeds, the thorns and the thistles. You have got to pull them up, burn them up and cleanse the land. And then you have got to get rid of this sourness and bitterness. You have got to drain your land.

I was staying with a farmer the other day and he took me to see a big acreage of land that he had recently bought. It had not been cultivated for centuries, and he showed me how he dealt with it. He drained it: he made a place for the poison to run out of it, to get rid of all the sourness in the land. Having done that, he put lime and other chemicals into it; you have got to do something to restore the productivity. And then he ploughed it up and harrowed it; he smashed and broke it up. Then he put seed into it, and rolled it, and the crop was beginning to appear.

What a wonderful parable of salvation in Jesus Christ! If Christ had not opened that 'drain' which we call Calvary, there would be no hope for any of us. What is Calvary? It is God's provision for draining the poison of sin out of us. It has got to be done; and Christ has opened the 'drain'. He has opened the way for the foulness, the sourness and the bitterness of sin to be taken out. He bore our sins in his own body on the tree. He has taken them away.

And then the Holy Spirit comes and begins to clear off the weeds and the rubbish and burn them. And he breaks up the land: he ploughs, harrows, smashes. Have you known conviction of sin under the Holy Spirit? That is what he does. He smashes. He breaks us down. Have you known the process? You will never produce the fruits of salvation unless you have been broken up, ploughed and harrowed by the Spirit.

And then these chemicals—the lime, the phosphates and so on—have got to be put in. Here they are in the word of God: the lime of the law, the chemicals of the epistles—these are the things that will increase production. And then, above all, is the seed of the word, the seed of life itself. He plants the seed of God's own life within the soul. And now there is a possibility again of productivity. 'This land ... is become like the garden of Eden.'

I am not just giving reign to my imagination; this is what Christ does. This is the whole story of the church and of Christian salvation. This is active; it works. It is not a theory. It is God acting in the soul. And as we have seen what needs to be done, we see that it has been done in Christ. And do you know the results? The garden begins to look tidy again. You no longer see thorns, thistles and other horrible weeds; they have gone! And there is order: I can see plots; I can see the paths again. When you walk into the garden, you say, 'What a neat, tidy garden!' Or you go round the farm and say, 'It's incredible! I remember what it was like. But look at it now!'

When you go into the country, have a look at the landscape. Look at the crop of hay. See the corn coming along. And go out again in a few weeks and see the corn beginning to change its colour. Look at the wheat in the field being wafted backwards and forwards in the breeze. See the glory, the beauty and the blending of the colour; is there anything more glorious, more magnificent, to look at than a well-cultivated farm or countryside? Tidy and ordered, it begins, as Ezekiel says, to look like the garden of Eden. 'Let the beauty of the Lord our God be upon us', says the psalmist (Psa. 90:17).

And then, of course, all this leads to a right use of our faculties. When Christ begins to farm your soul through the Holy Spirit, you will find that all that is in you, placed there by

God, begins to be used for the first time and in the right way. You will be aware of powers in yourself that you never knew you had: of interests, of possibilities, of likes. Everything that is ennobling and uplifting will begin to manifest itself.

Let me give you one of my favourite illustrations. There is a great hymn at the beginning of our hymnbook that begins with the magnificent arresting line, 'The God of Abraham praise.' It was written by a man called Thomas Olivers. He was once a tramp because of sin—because of drink in particular. But after his conversion he became not only a fine poet, but a great writer. That is what Christ does as Saviour. He removes the sin; he treats the soil; and the faculties begin to show themselves. So Paul, in Romans 6, can say, 'As ye have yielded your members servants to uncleanness and to iniquity unto iniquity; even so now yield your members servants to righteousness unto holiness' (verse 19).

That brings me to the crop. Oh, the contrast between the saint and the sinner! What is the crop? 'The fruit of the Spirit is love, joy, peace, longsuffering, gentleness, goodness, faith, meekness, temperance' (Gal. 5:22, 23). What a crop! In 1 Corinthians 13 we see the manifestation of life, of love, in the life of an individual—everything that is noble. Contrast the death of a sinner, which I described just now, with the death of a saint. What a difference! Oh, the crop of righteousness! Oh, the satisfaction of a life in Christ! Oh, the comfort in times of trouble! Oh, the consolation in times of need! Oh, the vision of eternity on a death-bed! Whatever the circumstances, there is a crop: something to rest upon, food, something to sustain the soul. That is the crop that results from salvation which is given by Christ.

And the most wonderful thing of all is that it increases and goes on increasing. The more you till the land, the more you get out of it. You are stimulating it to bring out what is in it. You are not exhausting it, as the other life did. You are bringing out the best. Notice Psalm 92:14: 'They shall still bring forth fruit in old age.' It produces, and it goes on producing. We grow in grace and in the knowledge of the Lord. We are in a process, according to the apostle Paul, which ends with this: 'unto the measure of the stature of the fulness of Christ' (Eph. 4:13). That is the growth. And the crop grows and is greater from year to year. It is astonishing! On and on it goes—until at last we arrive in the presence of God and we listen to his divine encomium, 'Well done, good and faithful servant.' He knows our works. 'Yea,' says the book of Revelation, 'their works do follow them' (Rev. 14:13). And we enter in upon our reward and upon the joy of the Lord.

What of your life? What of your soul? What of your productivity? I care not how old you are; you are old enough to produce some fruit. Is there any? Have you got anything you are proud of, anything you can lean upon when crisis, or some terrifying need that you had not thought about, suddenly comes upon you? Have you something to show, something you are proud of, that you can rest upon, something that holds you and helps you? Is there a crop, or is it sterile and barren, waste and useless? It must be one or the other.

If you feel that you are barren, sterile, waste and useless, go to God. Acknowledge it and confess it now. Ask him to have mercy upon you. Tell him the land is at his disposal. Ask him to begin the mighty operation. You will never ask him in vain. If you ask him and plead with him to do that, the Spirit will come and do his blessed work. You will feel your sin being drained away in Christ. The guilt will have gone. He will begin to deal with the very power of it. He will cleanse the land. And with the new life that he will put into you, you will begin to produce the fruit of the Spirit, to the glory of God, to your own enrichment, to the enrichment of all who know you, and to the joy even of the angels of God in heaven. Thank God for a gospel that can turn a wilderness into the garden of Eden; that can come to us, barren, miserable failures in life, and make of us saints producing graces to the glory of our blessed Lord and Saviour!

14. Saved by Grace Alone

And they shall say, This land that was desolate is become like the garden of Eden; and the waste and desolate and ruined cities are become fenced, and are inhabited. Then the heathen that are left round about you shall know that I the LORD build the ruined places, and plant that that was desolate: I the LORD have spoken it, and I will do it.

—Ezekiel 36:35, 36

I want to emphasize particularly verse 36: 'Then the heathen that are left round about you shall know that I the LORD build the ruined places, and plant that that was desolate: I the LORD have spoken it, and I will do it.' Here the prophet is really summarizing what he has been telling us throughout this important paragraph which begins at verse 16. And as the prophet sums up his message in these words, spoken to him by God that he might deliver them to the children of Israel, so we can by means of them, in this our last study, summarize what we have also been trying to say in our previous studies.

As we have been working our way through this momentous statement we have seen that what we are told here not only had an immediate direct and local application to the children of Israel, who were captives in Babylon because of their sin in their own land of Israel, but that it also is a marvellous preview of the Christian gospel. It is a most perfect description of the blessings of the Christian way of salvation.

And the summary in verse 36 is a vital summary because, as we are never tired of indicating, one of our great dangers, as we study the Scriptures and the gospel, is to miss the wood because of the trees. We do have to be concerned about details; the Scriptures are, and we must always follow the Scripture. But there is a danger that in following out the details, we forget the whole, which we must never do. We must always carry the whole in our minds as we are looking at the parts, for the parts are parts of the whole.

We are helped in this process by this verse. Here two of the great, vital principles that have been underlined in the entire passage are brought before us again.

First, there is the truth about sin. Sin is ultimately simply an attack upon God and upon his greatness and glory. We must never forget that. We are in danger of thinking of sin in terms of particular sins. We should and must do that, but that is not the real truth about sin. The essence of sin is that it is a refusal to give to God the glory that is due to his holy name.

Sin, let us never forget, started with Satan. There was a rebellion in heaven before anything ever happened on earth. It was that bright angelic spirit that first raised himself against God and disputed his Godhead. That is the origin of sin, and that was the essence of the attack upon God. The devil is the great antagonist of God; he hates the might, majesty and glory of God. And when he came and tempted man and woman in the garden of Eden, that was the line he adopted: 'Hath God said …?' It was the querying of God in every respect, an attempt to detract from the glory and greatness of God. That is the very essence of sin.

That is why we are reminded here, and especially thus at the end, that God is going to do all that he is going to do in order that the heathen may be silenced. What had the heathen been saying? We have already seen that when they looked at the children of Israel in the captivity of Babylon and saw the land of Israel desolate and uncultivated, and the cities all broken down, ruined and smashed, the heathen said, 'Ha! They talked about their God, that he was the only God, and they talked about his greatness and power. Well, if they had been right, they would never be in this position.' Sin always gives all who are opposed to God cause for rejoicing and jubilation. They are not interested in you and me as miserable sinners. What they are interested in is that God has been proved not to be what he claims to be. That is the essence of sin.

Whether we are Christians or not, we must grasp that idea and never forget it. It is not so much the particular shame of a particular sin, or that it makes beasts of men and women. No, it is that sin is spoiling God's handiwork, marring the image of God on men and women. And the forces of hell are rejoicing as they look at the chaos that has been introduced into God's glorious universe. That is why we have this emphasis in our verse: 'Then the heathen that are left round about you shall know ...'

The second principle fits in with that and comes out of it: salvation is primarily designed to vindicate God's character and to display the glories of God. This is something which you will find everywhere in the Scripture, from beginning to end. Remember how the apostle Peter puts it in 1 Peter 2:9, 10 when he reminds those Christian people, those strangers scattered abroad, that they are 'a chosen generation, a royal priesthood, an holy nation'—why? 'That ye should shew forth the praises of him who hath called you out of darkness into his marvellous light.' What is a Christian? A Christian is one who is designed to show forth the glories, the virtues, the excellences of God.

It is very important that we should always test our ideas of salvation in these terms. If our idea of what constitutes the Christian salvation does not do that, we can be quite sure that it is not the Christian salvation. It is important in an age like ours that we should learn how to draw these lines.

As I am never tired of reiterating, there are many, many agencies in this world that can, up to a point, duplicate the message of Christian salvation, just as the magicians of Egypt could, up to a point, do the things that Moses and Aaron did. Many agencies can indeed give you peace, happiness, joy, heal your body perhaps, or appear to give you guidance.

So is it not vitally important that we should have some differentiae that will for ever show us the difference between all these other agencies and the Christian gospel? Here it is: the Christian message always, everywhere, displays the glory of God. 'Then the heathen that are left round about you shall know that I the LORD build the ruined places, and plant that that was desolate: I the LORD have spoken it, and I will do it.' The wonderful thing about this Christian message is that, before it comes to you and me and our particular needs, it was planned in eternity to vindicate God's character, to justify God—not only before men and women, but also before all the powers of hell, Satan included, and to silence them for all eternity.

While we thank God for every subjective blessing that the Christian gospel gives, let us never forget the grand objectivity of it all. And let us see that God, over and above doing specific things for you and me, is doing something on the cosmic level, and to all eternity he is declaring that he is the Lord and that beside him there is no other.

Here, then, is our test for salvation. How does God do this? We can divide it up in the form of three principles, the first of which is this: this great and wondrous salvation is something that restores man to the position in which he was meant to be.

You will notice it is put in a very interesting pictorial manner here in our context. Again, remember the principle that in the Old Testament you generally get this blessing of God in salvation put in a material form. People knew they were blessed of God by the size of their flocks, the number of cattle in their herds, the number of children, and so on. God was condescending to the level of the people as they then were. This is but a picture of what God does spiritually in the New Testament in Christ. So this is how it is put here: 'And they shall say'—these are the heathen, the people who were scoffing at God, speaking when the salvation has taken place—'This land that was desolate is become like the garden of Eden.' They do not merely say, 'This land that was desolate has become as it was before those children of Israel were carried away.' No, they go further back, to the garden of Eden, right back to man as he was before the fall.

This is a tremendous principle that is of the very essence of the Christian faith. There are many who are outside Christ today because their whole idea of salvation is small and inadequate. But what a grand, vast, tremendous thing it is! God in salvation does nothing less than put man back to where he was before the fall ever came. If I may so put it, nothing less than that would become God. Our method is to patch things over, but God does not put a patch onto life. When God determined on salvation and decided to undo the effects and consequences of the fall, he decided to do the whole thing and to put man back where he was; nothing less.

That is the object of salvation: to restore man. Man, you remember, was made in the image of God. God stamped upon man something of himself. He made him upright. He made him stand erect upon his feet, not on all fours like the animals, as a sign of his lordship, his greatness, his likeness to God. He gave him a mind. He put him into correspondence with himself, that he might commune with him and enjoy his fellowship.

But, alas, as a result of the fall and sin, the image of God in man has been defaced and spoiled; not entirely lost, but marred. And there is man, a stranger away from home, driven out of the garden. So when God decided upon salvation he decided that there should be nothing less than the complete restoration of man to the place where he meant him to be.

You and I must realize that what this gospel offers is not merely forgiveness. Thank God, it does give us that—it is the first thing we all need, and without it we can have nothing further. But it does not stop there; that is the merest beginning.

What, then, does it offer to us? It offers to undo all the consequences of the fall. We can put it in these familiar terms: God sent his only Son, the Lord Jesus Christ, into this world. He sent him to the death of the cross, and he raised him again from the dead. Why? In order that you and I might receive the benefits of a full salvation. What is that? First and foremost, it deals with the guilt of sin. You have got to start with that. The bread and the wine of communion tell us that on a dark night when he was betrayed, Christ bore the punishment of our sins in his own body. They tell us that God made him to be sin for us who knew no sin, that we might be made the righteousness of God in him. 'Who his own self bare our sins in his own body on the tree, that we, being dead to sins, should live unto righteousness: by whose stripes ye were healed' (1 Pet. 2:24). That is essential.

If you had never realized that, I trust you do so now. You can never do anything about your sins. You cannot get rid of them; you cannot erase them. By living a good life from now on, you cannot undo what you have done. The guilt of sin is there. The record is in the books and you cannot undo it because you will still sin and still fail. There is only one way to deal with sins, and God has done it in Christ, who bore them and received their punishment, that God might freely forgive us.

But it also deals with the power of sin: the force of sin, the urge, as it comes from the devil and his suggestion. Had you realized that the gospel offers that? It offers to make a weakling strong. There are numerous examples of it in the Scriptures. Men and women who have been held in the bondage and shackles of sin can be liberated by Christ and are enabled to conquer their old enemies. There is power in this gospel to enable us to overcome our sins. We are not back in the garden of Eden unless we have the ability to resist.

It also deals with the pollution of sin. Let us never forget that sin pollutes us, vitiates our faculties, twists and perverts us, and spreads its ugly foul smear through the whole of our being. We need to be rid of that, and in Christ there is provision. The Holy Spirit is a gift of God who works within and his business and work is to get rid of this pollution and to make us eventually spotless, faultless, blameless and holy in the presence of God. Remember how Jude puts it: 'unto him who is able to keep [us] from falling, and to present [us] faultless before the presence of his glory with exceeding joy'.

Many do not realize this. They think of it all just in terms of forgiveness, and then we are left to ourselves. No, not at all; there is this blessed renewal, this new life, this new birth, this ridding of the power and pollution. But above all it brings us back to the place where we are given again the knowledge of God that we have lost and a restoration to a blessed fellowship and communion with God.

This is one of the most precious aspects of Christian salvation. Do you know God? Have you realized the presence of God? Adam was in communion with God before the fall. God came down into the garden and he spoke to man, and man was a companion of God. Man was made for knowledge and for communion with God. 'Thou hast made us for thyself, O Lord', said Augustine. But the fall has taken from us that direct, intimate knowledge of God.

Our conception of salvation is totally inadequate and incomplete unless we see in it this restoration to a living vital knowledge of God which is offered us in the gospel. 'We are made partakers of the divine nature', says Peter (see 2 Pet. 1:4), in order that Christ might dwell in our hearts by faith. 'This is life eternal,' says the Saviour himself, 'that they might know thee the only true God, and Jesus Christ, whom thou hast sent' (John 17:3). The elderly John writes in a letter in which he says, 'I am an old man. I'm going to die. But I am writing this to you that you may have fellowship with us, and truly our fellowship is with the Father and with his Son Jesus Christ' (see 1 John 1:3).

It is because so many who call themselves Christians know nothing about this that men and women outside have a false conception of Christianity. 'It's just forgiveness', they think — but that is not it. We are back in Eden; we are restored to where Adam was. In fact, I go further: we are put in a position beyond Adam in Christ.

In most of our hymnbooks a very wonderful verse is left out of Isaac Watts's hymn 'Jesus Shall Reign Where'er the Sun'. That verse includes the words:

Saved by Grace Alone

> In him the tribes of Adam boast
> More blessings than their father lost.

It is undoubtedly right. Not only are we forgiven and delivered from the power and the pollution; not only are we taken back into knowledge of God and into communion with God in a sense which was not true of Adam; but we are made the children of God in Christ Jesus: 'more blessings than their father lost.'

This is what the apostle Paul says about salvation to the Ephesians (he says it also to the Colossians): 'That ye put off concerning the former conversation the old man, which is corrupt according to the deceitful lusts; and be renewed in the spirit of your mind; and that ye put on the new man, which after God is created in righteousness and true holiness'—or, if you prefer it, 'is created in righteousness and holiness of the truth' (Eph. 4:22-24). Let us never think of salvation in any terms which are less than that.

Do you think that God would ever have sent his only Son out of heaven to do anything less than that? Hebrews 2:10 says, 'It became him'—that is, God—'in bringing many sons unto glory, to make the captain of their salvation perfect through sufferings.' In other words, when God decided to save man, he did it in a grand manner. It is not a part or in portions any longer; it is not a patch here and there, and man somehow put together. No, God made him anew in the image of his Son. Christ is the firstborn amongst many brethren. And we are to grow in the likeness of the image of his dear Son. So when God in salvation vindicates his own character, his own greatness and glory, he does it like that: by planning for us and holding out before us a complete, perfect, full salvation, with every vestige of the evil effects of the fall entirely done away with. What a glorious salvation!

231

But let me emphasize the second principle, which is that God's way of saving men is such that when he does it, it is clear to everybody that he has done it. 'Then the heathen that are left round about you shall know …'; 'And they shall say, This land that was desolate is become like the garden of Eden; and the waste and desolate and ruined cities are become fenced, and are inhabited.' The heathen, the scoffers, the unbelievers, stand back and say, 'What is this?' They can see that something has happened. They have to admit it.

This again is something tremendous that is emphasized in the Bible from beginning to end. There is nothing vague about God's way of salvation; there is nothing uncertain and indefinite about it. It manifests the power of God. Sometimes you read in the newspapers that somebody has discovered a great painting and nobody knows whose it is. They cannot quite make out the signature, or perhaps it is not there in full. And there is the great question: 'Is it one of the Masters, or isn't it?' There is a doubt about it. But the signature is always on the new man. If you want to know the difference between God saving a man and one of the counterfeits, this is the test: look for the signature. The work of God is unmistakable.

For example, remember what God did on the day of Pentecost at Jerusalem. There were the disciples, the apostles — ordinary, common, illiterate men, fishermen and artisans. Suddenly God sent his Spirit upon them, and the populace of Jerusalem, looking on, said, 'What is this?' They could see that something had happened, although they did not understand it.

Then the same thing happened shortly after, when Peter and John had healed a lame man at the gate of the temple. We are told that the authorities met together. They had heard the rumour about this, and they said, 'This is becoming serious and it's going to spread.' And we are told: 'Now when they saw the boldness of Peter and John, and perceived that they were learned and ignorant men, they marvelled; and they took knowledge of them, that they had been with Jesus' (Acts 4:13). They said, 'Whatever this is, it isn't these men. These are ordinary men: ignorant, illiterate, unlearned; but they've done this. What is it?' They were shaken and disturbed.

Then we read in the book of Acts of the conversion of Saul of Tarsus. He tells us himself that he had never been seen by face by the people in the churches of Galatia. 'All they knew,' says Paul, 'was this: that he who formerly persecuted us now preaches the gospel which formerly he persecuted and blasphemed' (see Gal. 1:23). It astounded everybody.

The book of Acts is full of this. You see the Philippian jailer, desperate fellow that he was, at one moment, in terror and alarm, pulling out his sword and on the point of committing suicide, a man in sin. Look at him in the next hour or two, rejoicing in God with all his house, praising the Saviour, joining the Philippian church. Everybody knew it.

Writing to the Romans, Paul says, 'First, I thank my God through Jesus Christ for you all, that your faith is spoken of throughout the whole world' (Rom. 1:8). 'Everybody,' he said, 'is talking about you. They've heard of you and what has happened to you.' This cannot be hidden. 'This land that was desolate is become,' said the heathen, 'like the garden of Eden.' God has done something here; look at the difference. That is God's way of salvation.

Again the apostle Paul, writing to the church of the Thessalonians, says precisely the same thing there: 'For from you sounded out the word of the Lord not only in Macedonia and Achaia, but also in every place your faith to God-ward is spread abroad; so that we need not to speak any thing. For they themselves shew of us what manner of entering in we had unto you, and how ye turned to God from idols to serve the living and true God' (1 Thess. 1:8, 9). God had done this thing and everybody could see it.

This therefore applies to you and me. When God does a work, it is unmistakable. The heathen can see it and have to bear their unwilling testimony to it. What do they see? They see that we have obviously got a new mind and a new outlook. When they see a man who lived for this world only becoming concerned about his soul and his relationship to God, they know it. They say, 'This man isn't as he was. He's got a new way of looking at things. He's got a new outlook and orientation.' 'If any man be in Christ, he is a new creature' (2 Cor. 5:17). He has the mind of Christ. What matters to him now is his soul and his eternal destiny. He is more concerned about that than about anything else. And those who used to know him say, 'But look here, you are not as you used to be. You used to come with us and were interested in our things. Why is it that you are no longer interested? You're not yourself; you're not the same.' What a testimony they pay to the work of God in your soul when they say things like that!

Have people said something like that to you? Have they noticed a great change in you? Are they aware that you have got a new interest and a new outlook? Have they become aware of a new life which is being lived by you? Do they see that, whereas you formerly failed and sinned with them, you no longer want to do so, and you no longer do so? When God acts in a man's soul, he gives him a new moral conception. He makes him hate things that he formerly loved, and love things that he formerly hated. He is washed, cleansed, sanctified, justified, in the name of the Lord Jesus.

Because it is God who does this work in a person's soul, it must manifest itself; it cannot help itself. Three hundred years ago an old Puritan said that when a man becomes a Christian, not only do all the people who knew him know it, but even his horse knows it. He is a new man with a new mind, a new heart—a heart of flesh that can feel. Instead of having the old stony heart, he is like Christ, and everybody must be aware of it. Is this evident in us? Do we show the signature of God in our lives? Are we manifesting his mighty handiwork in Christ Jesus in the new creation?

This brings me to my last point: not only is this work of God in salvation something that is evident to all others, but equally it is evident that it is God and God alone who has done it. What a difference there is between a man trying to pull himself together and to live a better life, and a man really being born again. Poor fellow, he realizes that he is going wrong. His wife perhaps chides him, and his children are weeping as they see him. He says, 'I must, I must pull myself together.' He makes a mighty effort of the will. That is one picture. The other picture is of God, the eternal Creator, taking the man and smashing him, and then moulding and making him anew, after the image of Christ. What a difference between morality and true Christian holiness! You see it at a glance!

This way of salvation is one that always displays the fact that it is God's work. What does it display? It displays the wisdom of God. If you do not see the wisdom of God in salvation, you are not looking at Christian salvation. Who but God could ever have thought of the way of salvation as it is in Christ Jesus? Man's way of salvation is always the way of philosophy: teaching, education, putting up a good example. He is doing it more than ever in this present century. He is trying to redeem humanity and himself by this method of human wisdom. But it does not work; it comes to naught.

But look at God's method. See the wisdom of it all. See the understanding, the mind, of the Eternal. And see not only his wisdom, but also his love, the fact that he ever looks upon us at all or bothers with us; the fact that he can look upon one who has rebelled against him and who metaphorically spat in his face and who hates him, and can do anything at all about him. Oh, the love of God displayed in this salvation!

And then see the power of God. There is a greater power needed here than for anything else. God made the world by the mere word of his fiat. He said, 'Let there be light', and there was light. But—and I say it with reverence—God could not undo the effects of the fall and of sin by a word. He gave his word to Moses; he gave him the law. But the law could not do it, in that it was weak through the flesh. But 'what the law could not do, in that it was weak through the flesh, God sending his own Son in the likeness of sinful flesh, and for sin, condemned sin in the flesh: that the righteousness of the law might be fulfilled in us, who walk not after the flesh, but after the Spirit' (Rom. 8:3, 4).

And how has God displayed all this? Where do I see the wisdom of God? Where do I see the love of God? Where do I see the power of God unto salvation? It is in Christ Jesus. There is God's mind, sending his only Son from heaven to earth, conceiving the incarnation. Man cannot conceive the incarnation. Though we have it revealed in the Scriptures and though we believe it, we do not understand it. Two natures in one person, unmixed: the mind boggles at it and is baffled by it. We stand with Paul and we say, 'Great is the mystery of godliness' (1 Tim. 3:16). No mind of man nor human ingenuity could ever have thought of that. The babe in the manger of Bethlehem is a manifestation of eternal wisdom. God saw man, human nature, fallen in sin and in vileness and hopelessness. And he said, 'This is what I'll do. I'll send down my own Son. He'll take human nature unto himself. He'll add it to himself and thereby he'll redeem it.' Oh, the wisdom, the blessed wisdom, displayed in the incarnation!

But follow it on: oh, the love involved in it, that God should send his only Son into a world like this, a world full of sin, shame, malice, bitterness, vileness and foulness; from the glory and the purity of heaven into an inferno like this! But he sent him. And the Son came. 'God so loved the world, that he gave his only begotten Son' (John 3:16).

But not only that; follow him as he goes along. See the wisdom of that divine human person baffling the doctors of the law at the age of twelve. See him in his public ministry. 'How knoweth this man letters, having never learned?' (John 7:15). 'Who is this?' Behold his power. The devil comes to him with all his might and malignity. Christ silences him with Scripture.

Above and beyond it all, standing in all its magnificence, glory and wonder, is the cross on Calvary—God's way of saving man.

> O loving wisdom of our God!
> When all was sin and shame,
> A second Adam to the fight
> And to the rescue came.

God's way was this: to take your sins and mine and to put them on Christ—in the garden secretly but supremely on the cross on high. Oh, the love of God! Oh, the mind and the wisdom of God that ever thought of it! Oh, the love of Christ that volunteered to do it and to bear it! And oh, in addition to that, the power of it all! He was great enough, holy enough

SAVED BY GRACE ALONE

and strong enough to take the sin, to bear the punishment, and yet, though dying, to rise again! He satisfied the law. He has conquered death and the grave! He has vanquished hell and every enemy. He rose victorious out of the strife and has gone back to heaven, where he is seated at the right hand of God's power and glory at this very moment. And it is by all that that God saves us.

Therefore, as Christians, we are witnesses and testifiers to this. I am what I am by the grace of God; and by nothing else. I am not here because I have pulled myself together or have exercised the will. I am a sinner saved by the grace of God. I am a weakling who has received the life of God in Christ. I am 'a debtor to mercy alone'. 'We are his workmanship, created in Christ Jesus unto good works, which God hath before ordained' (Eph. 2:10).

This is God's way, says Paul, and for this reason: 'that no flesh should glory in his presence' (1 Cor. 1:29); so that no one can stand up and say, 'I am what I am because I am what I am; because I have used my will power, because I've got a great brain. I've made myself what I am.' If you say that, you are not a Christian. God's way, says Paul, is one which has so been designed that no flesh should glory in his presence, but that all together should unite in singing, 'Worthy is the lamb that was slain and hath redeemed us to God.' That is what the Christian proclaims: that it is God's work. God's glory, God's wisdom and God's attributes have been manifested. And God in Christ has taken us and put us back where we were, in the garden of Eden, restored to the image of God and of Christ, standing before him as his children and heirs of his eternal glory.

> Unto him that is able to do exceeding abundantly above all
> that we ask or think, according to the power that now wor-

keth in us, unto him be glory in the church by Christ Jesus throughout all ages, world without end (Eph. 3:20).

'Then the heathen that are left round about you shall know that I the Lord build the ruined places, and plant that that was desolate: I the Lord have spoken it, and I *will* do it.' He *has* done it in Christ. Blessed be his holy name!

ABOUT THE PUBLISHER

THE Banner of Truth Trust originated in 1957 in London. The founders believed that much of the best literature of historic Christianity had been allowed to fall into oblivion and that, under God, its recovery could well lead not only to a strengthening of the church, but to true revival.

Inter-denominational in vision, this publishing work is now inter-national, and our lists include a number of contemporary authors, together with classics from the past. The translation of these books into many languages is encouraged.

A monthly magazine, *The Banner of Truth,* is also published. More information about this and all our publications can be found on our website or supplied by either of the offices below.

THE BANNER OF TRUTH TRUST

3 Murrayfield Road
Edinburgh, EH12 6EL
UK

PO Box 621, Carlisle,
Pennsylvania 17013,
USA

banneroftruth.org